CONTENTS

France's first world champion, Alain Prost

Colourful business: Italy's Michele Alboreto

GRAND PRIX

STUART SYKES AND ROGER MOODY

FOREWORD BY ALAIN PROST

BBC PUBLICATIONS

Published by BBC Publications
A Division of BBC Enterprises Ltd
35 Marylebone High Street
London W1M 4AA

First published 1986

© Roger Moody and Stuart Sykes 1986

ISBN 0 563 20471 0

Printed in England by
Redwood Burn, Trowbridge, Wiltshire

FOREWORD

My first drive in Formula One in Great Britain was alongside a British driver – that was with McLaren and John Watson in 1980. And in 1985, again in a McLaren, I won the World Drivers' Championship in Britain – so I have many good memories of Great Britain and many friends there.

All that time the BBC television motor-racing team of commentators and producers were recording my achievements. When I flew by helicopter into Brands Hatch early in the morning of 6 October 1985, the BBC were there to interview me – the only television crew present at that hour – and the same people were there again a few hours later to talk to me when I had become the Champion.

So I am very pleased to wish this BBC book 'Good Luck' and to send to all my fans and friends in Great Britain my best wishes – and thanks for their support.

A legend in his lifetime and beyond: Jim Clark, world champion in 1963 and 1965

INTRODUCTION

The aim of this book is to give motor-racing fans some insight into the complex world of Grand Prix racing, which is so much more than a few hours of fortnightly drama on our television screens. Sixty years have elapsed since international Grand Prix cars first thundered round a British circuit: what better pretext for a celebration than a Diamond Jubilee? It would be a brave man who set out to rival the marvellous yearbooks and technical tomes this colourful and complex sport brings forth, and that is not our ambition: the highly-informed follower knows where to look for the most detailed technical specifications, the most lavish driver biographies, the most complete race results, and a thousand more facts and figures from an activity that is a statistician's dream. Not an exhaustive catalogue, this – that is the province of the full-time writers who follow the Formula One circus round the world and are as much part of the scene as the best-known driver or team manager. More of an informed appetiser for the casual and enthusiastic 'wheels nut' who sometimes wonders what this mechanised mayhem is all about. No special passes required – just a little curiosity and a chair. Future chapters could look at a score of topics this book does not attempt to cover – other drivers, the politics of the game, the great names of the past and present – but for now this is an opener – a sort of 'setting-up' process. Isn't that how the cars come into being anyway? If it all goes wrong, please don't blame the drivers. . . .

Clark's arch-rival Graham Hill, the 1962 and 1968 world champion

CHAPTER ONE

ALL EXPLOSIVE AND VIOLENT ACTION

'Motor racing is a rather unusual sport.' With these laconic words the respected journal *Autocar* greeted the first motor race in this country to be dignified by the title 'Grand Prix'. Run at the famous Brooklands track in Surrey on 7 August 1926, it makes this year's Formula One race at Brands Hatch the diamond jubilee of Grand Prix racing in this country. Our friend from *Autocar*, probably its legendary Sports Editor, S. C. H. 'Sammy' Davis, was not entirely unimpressed: he enthused over race-winner Senechal from France as 'all explosive and violent action', thus setting the tone for what we have all come to expect and love in motor racing down the years. Not that Brooklands was the birthplace of the sport in its highest form: then, as in the decades that followed, Britain lagged behind the Continent of Europe – by the small matter of some twenty years.

For a great many casual observers, the history of Grand Prix is synonymous with the Drivers' World Championship, begun in the nicely-rounded year of 1950, and begun in Britain at that. This misconception shortens the intriguing story of Formula One by almost half a century. The Championship gave a tremendous fillip, of course, to a sport emerging from the post-war doldrums, but Grand Prix racing had been in existence since 1906. For us in Britain it may be diamond jubilee year, but motor racing itself started on the Continent almost a hundred years ago, and the road leading to Brands Hatch in 1986 has been long, full of surprising twists, and often dangerous to travel.

To France goes the credit for unleashing the sport on an unsuspecting world, at first with death-defying inter-city races such as Paris–Bordeaux–Paris in 1895. Given the state of the roads, the relative power of the vehicles involved, and the naïvete of those who turned out to watch, it was hardly surprising that accidents marred those early marathons. They were getting there, but not without unacceptable costs in human life as well as in other terms. With typical logic, the French realised the thing to do was confine their races to closed circuits. Hence the first-ever Grand Prix, organised on an early variant of what was to become arguably the single most famous stretch of tarmac in the world.

Take the N158 south out of Le Mans towards Tours and the Loire Valley and you are struck, just outside the Sarthe capital, by a sudden change in the road surface. You have just put wheels on the beginning of the fearsome Mulsanne Straight, where the monsters of modern endurance racing touch 230 mph in the world's best-known race, the 24 Heures du Mans. Not that such speeds were dreamed of in 1906: when the French decided they needed a larger share of the international action than the celebrated Gordon Bennett races gave them, they set out a circuit based on Le Mans totalling 64.12 miles, and required the cars to cover it twelve times in two days. Yes, twelve times: not for them today's two-hour sprints. The winning average speed, nonetheless, was a remarkable 62.879 mph, in a Renault proudly carrying the French banner. What do you mean, you've never heard of Ferenc Scisz? To that Hungarian gentleman goes the honour of seeing his name in the record-books as winner of the first-ever Grand Prix. Typically enough for the time there was no British entrant. In the beginning Grand Prix racing found it hard to break the parochial mould and go truly international.

Alas, no one was more guilty of keeping it on the island than the British. It was left to individuals – drivers and constructors – to take on properly-organised teams from France, Germany or Italy, while motor sport at home took shape as a fairly accurate reflection of the divisions of society.

Opposite, *First-ever world champion Dr Giuseppe Farina of Italy in action at Monaco in 1955, his last season;* top, *'Where did it go?' – old-style racing in pre-Grand Prix days at Brooklands;* bottom, *Programme cover for the first Grand Prix in Britain, Brooklands, 1926*

Brooklands, 1926: top, Senechal of France (Delage) *practises the chicane;* middle, Eyston's *Aston Martin ahead of Segrave's Talbot and Benoist's Delage;* bottom, 'The right crowd' *watching Halford in his Special lead Senechal at the same spot*

Five-times world champion Juan-Manuel Fangio of Argentina in a Maserati, Pescara, 1957

'The right crowd and no crowding.' With that élitist motto Brooklands, product of the entrepreneurial endeavour of one Mr H. F. Locke-King in 1909, was opened. By the time the first international Grand Prix graced the Surrey track little had changed. Patrons were advised, for example, that 'chauffeurs in livery will, as usual, be admitted free to the track'. Mention the year 1926 to most people and they will recall a period of national standstill, rather than a time to be bothered with new-fangled, high-speed modes of transport. Was it not the year of the General Strike? Britain was a nation divided: motor sport, still in its relative infancy and still a costly pastime, reflected those divisions, both in its hierarchical organisation and in the mere fact that it should prosper when the national life was visibly flagging.

But the 'right crowd' who flocked to Brooklands on 7 August that year were untroubled by such thoughts. For the first time the spectacle of the world's fastest automobiles speeding round the famous circuit was about to unfold. There were great names, such as H. O. D. Segrave, who was already well known for winning at the wheel of a Sunbeam in France and Spain. But the Weybridge track, a huge concrete dish permitting speeds that would not be out of place today, although some of its bite had been removed by the introduction of artificial chicanes to simulate corners, had the honour of bringing the latest technical masterpieces before the privileged few. Compare that rather eerie picture of Frenchman Senechal, eventual winner of the first historic race, practising in splendid isolation with the crowded scene at Brands Hatch or Silverstone today, and you have some idea of the gulf that separates us from those halcyon days . . .

Halcyon days? Not for the British motor-racing fraternity, such as it was. The two years that saw Brooklands play host to the Grand Prix world produced a sharp lesson in organisation, preparation and all-round professionalism. Moreover, the development of Grand Prix racing was under one of its regular shadows. Brooklands came to the international scene in what Grand Prix historian Rex Hays has called 'the peak year of designers' disillusionment', though a certain Monsieur Delage might take issue were he alive today. His purposeful cars ran away with both the 1926 and 1927 races, taking two of the first three places one year and producing a clean sweep the next. The Senechal/Wagner Delage number 14 had a race-winning average speed of 71.61 mph.

With the British entrants so comprehensively beaten, the reporters had time for quirkier things. English humour was unbowed, as a paragraph from *Autocar* in 1926 reveals:

Immediately after the race the winning partners had naturally but a single really strong impression, and this was the state of their feet, which, being cooked literally as brown as a well-done chicken, caused them considerable pain. Wagner, in particular, expressed himself in beautiful and forcibly expressive French coming straight from the heart. Senechal, thoroughly pleased at so great a success the first time he had officially formed part of the racing *équipe*, considered feet of secondary importance, though his description of their condition lost nothing in impressiveness for this reason.

Comedy apart, the lessons were there for the learning and Delage's 1–2–3 the following year, in what Hays thought 'probably the most outstanding example of speed plus reliability ever built', merely underlined them. So imperious was the French performance that one writer, as peeved as he was anonymous, refused to call the 1927 event a race. 'Rather did it prove a public demonstration of the high-speed reliability of French eight-cylinder cars', he complained. Not for the first – or last – time, the British motor industry came under attack for its refusal to back head-on competition with the giants of the Continent. Add to this general discontent motor-sport writer Doug Nye's conviction that 1927's Grand Prix was 'a one-make dominated 327-mile bore, and on this low note the 1½-litre Grand Prix Formula, which had promised so much, crept out of existence not with a bang, but with a long drawn-out whimper', and it is clear that something less than epoch-making sport was going on at Brooklands sixty years ago.

As Nye's acid comment reminds us, the world of Grand Prix racing is not content with one name: it also likes the title 'Formula One', conjuring up images of white-coated boffins beavering away in their laboratories to produce a curious species known as the Grand Prix car. Before bringing British Grand Prix history up to date, we must dwell for a moment on this question of 'formulae' and let the dictionary start us off on the right foot – or wheel.

The first definition of 'Formula' is a prescription for practical purposes: 'a set of words, definition, enunciation of principle in form of words, statement prescribed for use on some occasion'. This is precisely what has happened in Grand Prix racing: throughout the century there have been attempts to regulate the sport, tacitly or by public utterance, with rules usually governing engine capacities, vehicle weight and dimensions. The vital question, of course, is who does the uttering? Two dates stand out: in 1922 the Commission Sportive Internationale was set up to elaborate just what 'formulae' entrants into Grand Prix racing should follow; and in 1947 the unwieldy Association Internationale des Automobile Clubs Reconnus was transformed into the Fédération Internationale de l'Automobile. Since then, as we shall see, a further demarcation of responsibilities, between that body's sporting arm FISA and the increasingly powerful internal group known as the Formula One Constructors' Association, threatened to destroy the sport altogether until the famous Concorde Agreement got off the ground in the early 1980s.

Whoever has set down the 'formulae', these have usually been a challenge and a stimulus to the teams – something they had to circumvent by

Post-Grand Prix days at Brooklands: John Cobb airborne in 1937

whatever engineering sleight of hand they could contrive, and always with that simple but so often unattainable aim – speed plus reliability. Thus, for example, the rules for 1986 stipulate a maximum engine capacity of 1.5 litres. By a curious coincidence that is exactly the 'formula' that governed those Brooklands races sixty years ago, and one that has applied from time to time in the chequered history of Grand Prix racing. Only twelve years earlier, the 1914 French Grand Prix at Lyon, commonly held to be one of the great races of all time, was for cars with engine capacity of 4.5 litres. It attracted forty-one entries, from all major nations except the United States, and was a 1–2–3 triumph for Mercedes of Germany.

By the mid-twenties, then, there was an apparent drop of three litres in engine size. But the advent of supercharging – raising the pressure of air supplied to the engine's cylinders – had compensated for the decrease and heralded an era of high-speed racing unique in Grand Prix history. Forty years later, a similar revolution would be sparked off by Renault's introduction of the turbo-charged engine now omnipresent in Formula One.

Only after World War II did the specific notion of 'Formula One' emerge, when the new governing body decreed that cars might compete with 1.5-litre engines supercharged, or with 4.5-litre 'unblown' engines, the latter a throwback to Lyon in 1914. A certain Enzo Ferrari would make a great success of the latter category in a way that prompted direct British efforts to combat increasing Italian supremacy in the late forties and early fifties. That was Formula A, or One, with a Formula B, or Two, allowing for 500cc supercharged or 2 litres without supercharging, and the names have stuck ever since.

Even then, things did not remain static. By definition the Grand Prix world is fast-moving, and the fluctuations in Formula One were dizzying until twenty years ago. Between 1952 and 1954 the degree of international disagreement on what Formula One should be meant that in the end there was no agreement, and Formula Two was used instead. By 1954 a 500 cc/2.5-litre Formula, depending on the presence of supercharging or otherwise, was introduced. In 1961 it was back to 1.5 litres, with supercharging banned; but in 1966 came a return to 3-litre Formula One, which was also heralded as the 'Return to Power', and which has ended, curiously enough, only in time for the 1986 season.

More of that elsewhere: but it should be clear by now that 'Formula One' does not imply the manic workings of men in white, but a set of principles trying to regulate the performance and relative competitiveness of cars from the most cosmopolitan sources and enjoying the most disparate financial resources. In theory, at least, the Formula ensures a minimum of uniformity; more often than not it has been a valiant attempt by the powers that be to reduce speeds or costs, whichever seemed more practical.

England's talented Dick Seaman drove for Mercedes at Donington in 1937 and 1938

So far, it should be noted, no effort has succeeded in reducing significantly the awesome performances the Grand Prix car can achieve. Like all institutions, Grand Prix is so familiar to us – especially through the power of television – that it seems always to have existed, always bound by the same principles. Nothing could be farther from the truth. Finding the right formula to govern this 'explosive and violent action' has often been a long process of internal and international wrangling, with bitterness giving way to good old compromise on more than one occasion.

But to get back to the action . . . Despite the enduring popularity of club racing and other meetings, and some truly remarkable assaults on speed records, Brooklands never again enjoyed a Grand Prix in the way we now understand them, and sadly much of the splendour of that cradle of British motor racing is now joined with the Surrey dust. It would be some years before the big boys came back to play in mainland Britain, and when they did overseas drivers would again walk away with the glittering prizes. The scene by then had switched north to Donington Park near Derby, and if the Grands Prix at Brooklands had disappointed home spectators, the middle years of the thirties produced motor racing at a pitch beyond anything seen before – and possibly since.

Thanks to the enterprise of one Mr Fred Craner, the circuit at Donington,

Oops! Seaman again in a slightly crumpled car on the same circuit

with its famous Melbourne hairpin, Starkeys Bridge, Coppice Corner and all, staged 'Grands Prix' in 1935 and 1936, when Britain's Richard Shuttleworth and the immensely talented Dick Seaman triumphed – in Italian Alfa Romeos. By this time the 'monoposto', or single-seater, was giving the Grand Prix car something like the lines with which we are now familiar, but not until 1937 did Craner's vision of a truly international, top-flight Grand Prix materialise. When it did, it brought cars to Donington Park that rank among the greatest racing machinery ever produced.

With the help of state funds set up by Hitler, the German teams of Mercedes Benz and Auto Union – with engineering input from a certain Dr Porsche – built cars to eclipse the finest that France or Italy could throw at them. This was the time of the clash of the Titans, not only in the cars but in the men who drove them. Nuvolari of Italy, Germany's Lang and Rosemeyer, and Caracciola, German despite his name, and known as 'Der Regenmeister' because of his uncanny car control in the wet, were names to grace the pages of any history of Grand Prix greats. 'The spectacle of those gigantic cars of 1937,' wrote the great motor-sport historian Laurence Pomeroy, 'their hurtling accceleration, and the triumph of man over machine when cornering, seems unlikely ever to be surpassed.' Twice in a row, before the machinery of Fascism was geared to other conquests, Auto Union headed home Mercedes as Donington looked on and held its breath.

Where, we may ask, was the British effort at the time? Why could the Seamans of this world find no home-manufactured machinery to project them round the tight turns, over the hair-raising hills and along the straights at Donington? The answer, as a decade earlier, was – nowhere. Still looked on as a minority interest, motor racing was shunned by the major manufacturers. But the world changed in those years as surely as it would in the course of war, and when racing began again there was a new determination in Britain to put right those years of missed or neglected opportunity. In Doug Nye's words, that second display by the Titans was 'a day which put a true perspective on England's parochial form of motor racing, and a day which planted a seed in English hearts which was to bear fruit twenty years later'.

Six Britons have had it, though it has visited these shores ten times in all. Our closest rival is Argentina, but only one name from that country ever laid claim to it, and the threat from South America is now Brazilian. It has travelled to the Antipodes, the United States and Finland, but surprisingly the Austrians have taken it more often than the Italians. 'It', of course, is not

Donington start-line, 1937

14.

Top, *Donington swan-song: Nuvolari's Auto Union leads away in 1938;* bottom, *Fangio in rueful pose;* opposite, *Crystal Palace in 1937 drew big names too, such as Villoresi* (right) *and Italian friends*

a disease but an honour – the Drivers' World Championship, which so many associate so closely with the history of Grand Prix racing, but which was introduced only in 1950. Before it came into being, however, there was this problem of the cars: when would Britain produce one capable of beating the rest of the world?

When Grand Prix racing began again in earnest after the war, British eyes were trained on the Lincolnshire village of Bourne, from which would come

the home-made answer to our international motor-sporting prayers – or would it? BRM: the initials roll off the tongue as crisply as an exhaust note; the name itself, British Racing Motors, is not so much a simple description as a warning to the rest. That was how it seemed, at least, as 1950 approached and this family-based concern set about restoring – or creating – British fortunes in the Grand Prix world.

To combat the dominance of the Alfa Romeos, BRM, drawing its resources from the engineering-based wealth of the Owen family and Louis Stanley, set out to exploit the skills of two gifted men. Raymond Mays had achieved some success with his ERA – English Racing Automobiles – machines in the *voiturette* category, on which British efforts were concentrated in the late thirties, but now there were bigger fish to fry – almost literally, as it at first turned out. As for Peter Berthon, he blazed a trail which British expertise has followed ever since, as Louis Stanley explains: 'Peter Berthon was quite in a class of his own, one of the first really great designers. He and Raymond Mays were like a pair of bookends. But there was introduced a feeling that money was limitless: when that happens, the urgency and astuteness that come from working to a tight budget are lost.' What set out with the admirable aim of making an all-British assault on Grand Prix racing foundered, then, on the rock of complacency, compounded by that evil of democracy, government by committee. BRM was run by a Trust, its individual members given to fits of pique when their views were rejected. The net result was what Stanley candidly calls, in his book *The BRM Story*, 'the most enigmatic, controversial car in Grand Prix history'.

If money was abundant and the designer so gifted, why did this fabulous creature fail? Basically because of the engine. A sophisticated V16 unit designed to extract the maximum from the 1.5-litre supercharged Formula then in force, it was unable to provide the power progressively, and so – like some of the recent turbocharged engines in their development stages – was quite unpredictable and awkward for the driver to control. In short, the BRM of which so much was expected made only one full Championship appearance. After an embarrassing failure to get away in the 1950 British Grand Prix, they at least finished the next year's race, though the fish fried in cockpits overheating like miniature kilns were hapless drivers Parnell and Walker, finishing respectively five and six laps adrift of the winning Ferrari driven by Froilan Gonzales.

A decade later, BRM – much revised, its power unit simplified – would regain self-respect by winning the World Constructors' Championship of 1962. As Stanley says, 'Everything was done from scratch – the long way of

Opposite, *Silverstone grid, 1948: Johnson's ERA (no. 15) with Parnell's Maserati (no. 6), Rolt's Alfa-Aitken (no. 29), the Lago-Talbot of Rosier (no. 3) and others*

Top, 'Don't tell me that!' Stirling Moss at Silverstone, 1959; bottom, Graham Hill preparing to tell the world in a BBC broadcast in 1974

Hill was 'Mr Monaco': here he is in typical action at a circuit where he won five times

carrying out an expensive exercise. But when you achieve success there is a measure of satisfaction beyond what the kit merchant can have.' What made early disasters even more galling was the success story of one member of the BRM committee who grew tired of the bickering, decamped, and set about making his own team of world-beaters.

Tony Vandervell – 'a go-getter, no time for red tape', in Stanley's recollection – was a millionaire bearing manufacturer to whom would fall the historic honour of carrying off the first-ever Constructors' World Championship, in 1958. Using 'cast-off' Ferraris at first, his Vanwall team would run in twenty-eight Grands Prix, claim seven pole positions, and win nine races in the years 1957–8. How much of that success was due to one driver in particular is difficult to assess, but it seems undeniable that England's Stirling Moss was the greatest driver never to win the world title. In 1957 – the fruit of Doug Nye's twenty-year seed – Moss and Tony Brooks gave the Vanwall its first World Championship win in front of a jubilant Aintree crowd. The following year Moss and Brooks had three wins each en route to giving

Vandervell his heart's desire, a feat since emulated no fewer than eighteen times by British-based teams, culminating in McLaren's second successive world championship in 1985. 'Vanwall's success', reflects a wry Louis Stanley, 'made Lent seem like a jolly period as far as we at BRM were concerned! But you had to have a sense of humour as well. Everything was done in a spirit which today is lacking: it's really all a Formula One wheeler-dealer exercise now.'

But BRM's day was to come. If Moss was the making of Vanwall, he had a counterpart where the Bourne outfit was concerned in Graham Hill. The late Hill, twice world champion and only man to win the Monaco Grand Prix five times, described by Stanley as 'very nearly a classic driver', claimed his first win for BRM at Zandvoort in 1962 (also the circuit of James Hunt's first Grand Prix win in the Hesketh in 1975), three seasons after Sweden's Joakim Bonnier had laid the ghosts of BRM's past with victory for the marque on the same Dutch circuit. In 1962 Hill won four races out of nine and was placed in four others on the way to his first World Championship. He would have six years to wait for his second, but when it came it was perhaps a greater measure of the man's character: stepping into the breach

Clark's last win, South Africa, 1968. Three months later he was killed at Hockenheim

when the great Jim Clark was killed, Hill, by then the Scot's teammate at Lotus, responded with wins in Spain, Monaco – of course – and Mexico, to put some balm on the wounds Clark's death had opened in the motor-racing world and at Lotus in particular.

Was Jim Clark the greatest Grand Prix driver of all time? The *Times* obituary said so unashamedly; *Autosport* was more measured but got the tone just right:

Clark's name was a household word, and to hundreds of thousands of people who knew nothing of motor racing it stood for skill, courage and sportsmanship. Equally, the incalculable number who never knew him but watched him race from grandstands and spectator enclosures, and followed the international racing circus in the motoring press, will feel a sense of personal loss.

To call Jim Clark the last of the great amateurs in Grand Prix racing is no insult: while a consummate professional, and one whose habit of winning motor races made him latterly a tax exile, his style of driving and his way of talking about the sport were those of a man who did it out of love. It was the great Argentine driver Juan-Manuel Fangio, five times world champion before Clark came on the scene, who said: 'Speed creates a sensation of

Laid-back, arms straight: Maestro Clark enjoying himself as only he could

being alive, more than alive.' To see Jim Clark in action was to have that feeling joyously confirmed.

Between 1960 and 1968 Clark won twenty-five World Championship races out of only seventy-two starts. Champion in 1963 and 1965, he was denied the title in 1962 and 1964 only by cruel luck. His victory at Kyalami in his last Grand Prix, on New Year's Day in 1968, showed him on the threshold of a third triumph. He drove all kinds of cars, from Jaguars with the Border Reivers to the finest Formula One machinery of its day. It was in a footling Formula Two race at Hockenheim on 7 April 1968 that disaster – so far unsatisfactorily explained – befell him. Jim Clark would have been fifty in this diamond jubilee year of Grand Prix racing in Great Britain.

Graham Hill must have hated the Scots! After virtually a decade in which his hard work was so often eclipsed by the natural genius of Clark, along came John Young Stewart to assume his compatriot's mantle of greatness. The year of Jim Clark's death was a watershed in another respect, in that it marked the advent of unfettered commercialism into motor racing, and many are those who feel Clark would have been desperately ill at ease in the glare of publicity the sponsors' contracts brought. Not so Stewart, who was to take over as his country's – and the world's – finest exponent of the Grand Prix art. Jackie Stewart won his first Grand Prix as Hill's teammate at the wheel of a BRM at Monza in 1965, the last European race of that particular variation on the 1.5-litre Formula. For the next eight years he dedicated himself to building a Formula One career that brought unprecedented rewards, exploited all the business acumen of the pawky Scot, and sowed seeds the astute JYS has been able to harvest to this day.

Above, *Jackie Stewart's first win for BRM at Monza in 1965, Hill and Clark in pursuit;* opposite, *The smile of a triple world champion*

Unlike Hill, Stewart quit while ahead, albeit in tragic circumstances. The 1973 United States Grand Prix was to be his 100th and last, but Stewart withdrew when his teammate and protégé, François Cévert of France, was killed in an accident during practice at Watkins Glen, NY. Stewart took twenty-seven wins in those ninety-nine races, a total only France's Alain Prost looks like threatening in the foreseeable future.

The other factor Stewart had in common with Clark, apart from their origins, was a half-share in one of those partnerships that sport occasionally throws up – and which, when it does, rewrite the history books. Clark, first of all, was the driving arm of Colin Chapman's unique engineering genius. When Chapman was starting to construct the Lotus team that would earn a reputation second to none for innovation, consistency and flair, he recognised in Clark a talent to exploit the design skills that would make Chapman's cars monarchs of all they surveyed and create landmark after landmark in Grand Prix history. The easy skills of Clark and the relentless energy of Chapman forged what must surely stand as the sport's most successful partnership, one that took British ability to all corners of the Formula One empire, conquered America in the 1965 Indianapolis 500, and built a legend nothing can diminish. Between 1963 and 1978 Lotus took the Constructors' Championship seven times, Chapman's fertile brain coming up with idea after idea – the first monocoque in succession to tubular-frame

Craftsman at work: the brilliant Lotus team manager, Colin Chapman

construction for the Grand Prix car, innovations in aerodynamic chassis construction, the brilliant Lotus 25 of 1962 which Bill Boddy called 'the father of all subsequent Grand Prix cars', the Lotus 49 and 72 – in an endless stream of answers to the practical problems posed by that constant equation: speed plus reliability.

Stewart's partnership was rather different, for the man he worked with has only one Constructors' Championship to his credit and his team's fortunes have fluctuated alarmingly in the years since 1973, when Stewart called it a day. But Ken Tyrrell was astute enough in the first instance to harness Stewart's driving skills to his own managerial ability, first running the French-backed Matra team in 1968 and 1969, then in his own Formula One venture from late 1970 on. Three times the Scot took the sport's highest honour, in 1969, 1971 and 1973, the middle year making Tyrrell Constructors' Champion in his first full season of running his own Formula One team. It seems clear that there was a different balance in this relationship than there had been between Clark and Chapman: Stewart's skills had a greater say in determining the success of Tyrrell's cars, as is proved by the team's relative lack of success in the years that followed Stewart's retirement.

Since the Clark–Chapman or Stewart–Tyrrell days, when a clear and warm relationship existed between driver and constructor, no similar pair-

Chapman with the 1978 world champion Mario Andretti, whose Lotus won six times that year

Driving force: top, *The Ford-Cosworth's début in 1967 at Zandvoort with Lotus en route to 155 wins;* above, *The 1977 Renault that began the turbo revolution;* left, *Frenchman Jean-Pierre Jabouille in the 'national' car*

ing has exercised such dominance over the Formula One world, though the likeable American Mario Andretti did a wonderful job with and for the Lotus manager in 1978, winning six races en route to World Championships both for himself and for the constructor. There was also the case of Austria's Niki Lauda and Ferrari, whose fortunes he revived in 1975 when the world titles went to Lauda and the famous scarlet cars, but we still wait for the next natural successors to those all-British combinations of the sixties and early seventies. Nigel Mansell bids fair to do the trick at Williams, but more of that later (pp. 51ff).

Before we leave the Clark–Chapman subject, one other crucial factor has to be borne in mind: engines. In conjunction with a former Lotus employee called Keith Duckworth, whose latest creation was revealed to a waiting world in 1986, Chapman was instrumental in the development of the most successful racing engine of all time. Twenty years ago the 'return to power' might have been better described as 'the discovery of power', and the man to discover it, in the shape of the Ford-Cosworth V8 Formula One engine, was Duckworth. Once Chapman had persuaded Ford to fund its development, the engine became an irresistible force in Grand Prix racing from the moment of its spectacular entry into the arena. The Ford-Cosworth earned ten World Constructors' Championships, powered twelve drivers to their titles and repaid many time over Ford's faith in Chapman and his partners. 'The chief beneficiaries of their long association', wrote John Blunsden in his splendid book *The Power to Win*,

have been the ever increasing number of people for whom motor racing has been their livelihood and the countless thousands of spectators for whom the sight of battle between professionally run teams of well matched cars and drivers continues to be of such absorbing interest. They should all be grateful for that day when Ford and Cosworth sat down together and decided to 'do an engine'.

Why so? Because the Ford-Cosworth, when it was made available not solely to Lotus but to all interested parties, put teams on a more equal footing and created the conditions in which close racing was possible. The engine, installed in the Lotuses of Clark and Hill, made a winning début at Zandvoort in 1967. Since then it has won no fewer than 155 Grands Prix, although the last was in 1983 when Michele Alboreto's Tyrrell took the chequered flag at Detroit. Until its arrival, manufacturers like BRM or the indefatigable Ferrari had gone their own way and had it their own way, though smaller independent engine firms such as Coventry Climax or Brabham Repco had enjoyed temporary success.

The next great landmark in engine technology would arrive in 1977, when French giants Renault installed a turbocharged power unit in their own Formula One car and launched an attack on the World Championship that ended in paradox: the failure of that team to exploit engines with which other cars were able to win races, and the withdrawal of Renault's team from Formula One racing. Their engine, however, was instrumental in ending the twenty-year era of the Ford-Cosworth. With the 1986 regulations stipulating the use of 1.5-litre power units, with supercharging permitted, the ten-year rise of the turbo is now complete. We need only consider the success of the Tag-Porsche engine in the all-conquering McLarens of 1984 and 1985 to appreciate how far supercharging has come since those far-off days at Brooklands. The engine was responsible for eighteen Grand Prix wins in those two seasons. With the Japanese Honda units now so explosively quick and reliable for Williams, who won the last three races of 1985, the all-out speed of the BMW engines used by Brabham, Arrows and Benetton, and the latest Renault technology powering a number of teams including Tyrrell and Lotus, a new era of competitiveness – speed plus reliability – has dawned. Curiously enough, the British Grand Prix again finds itself at the centre of the historical stage, for it was at the 1977 Silverstone race, won by James Hunt's McLaren, that the Renault turbo engine first raced.

Mention of Silverstone reminds us that only two circuits now host Grand Prix racing in Great Britain, though Donington Park holds out hopes of bringing the modern Titans back to the East Midlands. Once Aintree had dropped off the list in 1962 – albeit after the historic races of 1955 and 1957 – it was left to a former grass-track motorcycle venue in Kent to share the international limelight with Silverstone. The last man to win a British Grand Prix at Aintree was Jim Clark: he is also the only Briton ever to have won a British Grand Prix at Brands Hatch, scene of this year's race.

Above, *Clark leads the first Grand Prix off at Brands Hatch in 1964;* opposite, *John Watson (McLaren), last home winner of the British race at Silverstone in 1981*

Clark's Brands success came in 1964, the inaugural Grand Prix meeting, when the world champion's Lotus came home ahead of Graham Hill's BRM. The Kent circuit held its first race meeting in 1950 – when Silverstone was playing host to the first-ever Drivers' World Championship Grand Prix. A certain S. Moss won all five of his races at a June meeting at Brands Hatch in 1950, while another early racer on the embryonic Kent circuit was Mr Bernie Ecclestone, now king-pin of the Formula One Constructors' Association. Since Clark's triumph – he was also first to do the ton at Brands the next year – the circuit has become the busiest in the world, and Britain boasts two of the world's very finest. Silverstone is flat and super-quick, Brands all swoops and bends and a different challenge entirely to the drivers' skills. Both enjoy an enviable reputation for well-organised racing, even if the seventies saw the British Grand Prix marred by incident and acrimony. At Brands in 1976, for example, a first-lap pile-up involving the Ferraris of Niki Lauda and Clay Regazzoni left James Hunt's McLaren badly damaged. When he was excluded from the re-start an unprecedented crowd display brought a swift change of heart, but though Hunt was inspired to 'win' the race he was subsequently disqualified.

No matter: he was still crowned world champion at the end of the year, and remains the only Briton to achieve the feat since the days of Stewart – despite the efforts of men like John Watson, whose storming drive to win the British Grand Prix for McLaren at Silverstone was the highlight of 1981. Besides Clark, Hill and Stewart, only two others have taken the Drivers' World Championship for Britain: the enigmatic Mike Hawthorn, contemporary of Moss, who raced with great success, for Ferrari in particular, and took the 1958 title for the Italian marque by a single point from his luckless compatriot; and John Surtees, only man to move from world championship success on two wheels to similar exploits on four, again with Ferrari in 1964.

Mind you, no one who was present at the 1985 European Grand Prix at Brands Hatch will forget the sight of Britain's Nigel Mansell taking the chequered flag in his Williams for his first-ever World Championship win. It was one of the great moments of a marvellous sporting summer, and as Brands in 1986 creates a new precedent by staging World Championship races in five consecutive seasons – three British and two European Grands Prix – all home supporters hope Mansell can emerge as a genuine championship contender.

Clark, Stewart and Hill stand apart in their ability to win more than one title and in the consistent quality of their contribution – Hill, for example, drove in a staggering 176 Grands Prix. In that, they are typical of what Britain, since those dark early days, has achieved in Formula One racing. In latter years

Opposite, *Nigel Mansell, Williams' hero at Brands Hatch in 1985* the drivers at the pinnacle may have been Brazilian, Austrian, Finnish or French, but a massive percentage of the technical input to Formula One is British, with no fewer than nine of the 1986 teams based to all intents and purposes in this country.

Later chapters will examine why that should be, but it is time to consider that most absorbing creature, without whom there would be no racing to enthuse over: the Grand Prix driver. To introduce him, a word from nearly sixty years ago, written by the doyen of motor-sport writers, 'Sammy' Davis:

The truth is that motor racing can only be enjoyed by those who understand what they are looking at, whereas the uninitiated spectator really wants to see a sort of circus. If motor racing is to become a circus, the whole thing will have to be reconsidered and put on an entirely commercial basis. Drivers will have to be paid as performers; indeed some of them are clamouring for it now. To give the crowd thrills the driver would have to become something between the music-hall sea-lion and an acrobat.

That view was expressed in 1927. What do the 'sea-lions' in the class of '86 have to say for themselves?

CHAPTER TWO
DRIVING AMBITION

Few sports present such a wide range of individuals as modern Grand Prix racing. From the lazy grace of Brazil's Nelson Piquet – one of his most enthusiastically pursued pastimes is sleep – to the Australian earthiness of Alan Jones, the variety of character and attitude is remarkable when you remember we are talking about some thirty men with one common objective – the Drivers' World Championship.

Take the four Britons who began the 1986 world championship in Rio in March. Most widely tipped for success was Nigel Mansell, the 'Birmingham Boy' who so proudly boasts of his 'living complex' on the Isle of Man, and devotes his time almost as single-mindedly to improving his golf as he does to paring hundredths of a second off the lap times of his Williams on the track. In comparison with race-winning veteran Mansell (Brazil was the seventy-fifth Grand Prix of the 31-year-old's career), the three others were Formula One rookies.

Martin Brundle, a 26-year-old director in the family motor business in King's Lynn, was starting the long haul back to the top after losing many months to the aftermath of a Dallas accident. Undoubtedly quick, he has yet to be seen in a really competitive car (see Chapter 4), but with the arrival of Data General to the Tyrrell team and the substantial increase in resources, Brundle's testing skills look perfectly harnessed to the team's needs. Despite early-season mishaps, one of which – practice in Jerez – he attributed to his own error, Martin's forthright, friendly nature masks his tremendous determination to get to the top. The Data General livery in black and white does not imply an 'all or bust' attitude. Brundle's canniness belies his years.

Then there's John Colom Crichton-Stuart. The French and Italians, and particularly the Americans, will love the Earl of Dumfries but the sophisticated Scot prefers the somewhat less sophisticated name Johnny Dumfries. A newcomer to Formula One this season, Johnny wants to be ranked with the rest of his driving colleagues and to be treated on his own not inconsiderable merits. A motor racer with traditional training – he has performed in almost all types of car – he and his wife, Freddie, are an engaging double act. Johnny, slightly shy, very calm, yet almost boyish has in his wife a vivacious partner whose commitment to his success almost exceeds his own! Dumfries' 'junior' role to Senna at Lotus should not,

Rising star Martin Brundle keeps it tight at the 1986 Spanish Grand Prix

however, be interpreted as a willingness to be second – he is a winner and intends to succeed in Formula One. In terms of motivation his reasons may well be simple – driving quickly comes naturally.

The fourth Briton is the 'Doctor in the House' – Jonathan Palmer. The qualified GP forsook his healing knowledge to go racing full time in 1981 but having another career to fall back upon did not make him the new 'pacemaker'. Injections of another sort were needed.

'God, the agony of that winter just about exceeds anything in my life!' The lament is Palmer's, pointing up the relevance of the first question most people would like to ask a Grand Prix driver: why does he do it? The stresses Jonathan recalls were not even those of a racing-car cockpit, but the different pressures of the marketplace. The product: Dr Jonathan Palmer, British Formula Three champion of 1981, Formula Two champion of Europe two seasons later, the medical man with the most determined bedside manner in the business – a driving talent with the ambition to win a world championship. Still not thirty, Palmer in that winter of 1983–4 was one of the hottest properties on the fringes of the Formula One scene. Surely team managers would be falling over themselves to secure his signature on a Grand Prix contract? It was never quite that simple, as Palmer in his matter-of-fact fashion recalls: 'Many people thought my getting into Formula One was almost a formality; the only thing left to chance would be how good a seat I got. In fact I wasn't in nearly as favourable a position as that.'

Top, *Brundle, Palmer, Dumfries, Mansell;* bottom, *Nelson (Piquet) turns a blind eye*

What ensued reflects a side of the modern racing-driver's life the public rarely glimpses: the Grand Prix ace as door-to-door salesman, albeit with one of the fastest company cars on earth. Luckily for Palmer, he had the confidence to sell himself in the most convincing terms. The first hurdle was the shortage of seats available in the sport's highest echelon: with only a relatively small number of teams involved, and only twenty-six places to be filled on each Grand Prix grid, space for newcomers is at a premium. Palmer had two apparent options, one of which – with Ken Tyrrell, long renowned

Top, *Brundle, 1986;* bottom, *Different colour, different car, same Tyrrell team in the USA, 1984*

A driver's life is clearly signposted: Keke Rosberg at Detroit in 1984

Hot shoe of his day: Stirling Moss in 1952 receives personal attention

as a team manager willing to nurture up-and-coming talent – was effectively removed when the Ockham team went though their own sponsorship crisis. That left John MacDonald, whose Bicester-based RAM team is one of those who mean so much to motor racing even if in Formula One they more often than not start from the back of the grid. There was one small problem: money. MacDonald, who had offered Palmer a drive in 1981 but failed to woo him away from his F3 commitments, was keener than ever to run the doctor in one of his cars. All Palmer had to do was bring along £250,000!

Palmer makes the raising of this substantial sum sound comparatively easy. 'I just went through a whole load of my previous contacts, really. My whole time that winter was spent telephoning people, writing to people, putting together sponsorship proposals, organising and attending meetings. I must have had a hundred wasted meetings . . .' But somehow things came together and his efforts raised a great part of the sum required – though by no means all. 'I ended up having to borrow £100,000' is the cool admission. 'But I took the view that I just had to get into Formula One that year, and I was *so* committed down the line.'

The main reason for his haste was simple enough. In motor racing, as in most sports and businesses, optimum timing is crucial. 'Obviously I did have some advantage', says Palmer, 'in being a driver who had a hot name at the time. Now that doesn't happen very often to very many of us, and when it does you've got to try and carry it on. You're on the crest of a wave, and you've got to make sure it carries you somewhere. But I had to do an awful lot of hard work to capitalise on it.'

Even when the money had been begged and borrowed, it looked for a moment as if it might all have been in vain. 'In the meantime,' continues

Top, *Palmer made it into F1 in 1984 at the wheel of a RAM;* bottom, *The man with the most driving ambition of all, the brilliant Ayrton Senna*

Palmer, 'RAM had done a deal with the young French driver Philippe Alliot and I thought that was that. But then John MacDonald said, "Hang on a minute: if you can get that sort of money, we can make the effort to run two cars."' That was how things turned out, though in the end it was very much a last-minute affair. 'I signed a contract with John four days before the Brazilian Grand Prix, and went to my first race of the season having done no testing, never having driven the car, only just absorbing the fact that I was in Formula One. But at least I *was* just that. I had got to the first race of the 1984 season and I was *there*.'

And where precisely was 'there'? Picture the scene, after all: a hot

Opposite, *The unmistakable yellow helmet of Senna at the wheel;* above, *Brundle uses a special cap to keep a cool head in the searing heat of Rio*

summer afternoon in Brazil (for the 1986 race it was 96° Fahrenheit in the pit lane), or for that matter France or Belgium or Kent. In that heat a man swathed from head to toe in fireproof clothing allows himself to be strapped into a machine that surrounds him with some fifty gallons of high-octane fuel. Once set in motion, that machine becomes a projectile capable of speeds we ordinary mortals can only begin to imagine. This activity is pursued, for the most part, on tracks no wider than the average main road. When the projectile sets off, it is surrounded, at first in the tightest of formations, by twenty-five others, usually with a tricky little corner placed sadistically at the end of the first straight. The slightest error, human or mechanical, is liable to bring any one of these machines into high-speed contact with an unforgiving surface: banking, barrier or even concrete fence. At full speed such incidents can be, in the graphic phrase of Grand Prix veteran John Watson, 'like a fly being swatted against a wall'.

What drives a human being to pursue this seemingly inhuman activity? Why strain every sinew to break into Formula One? Why spend a winter off the track raising fabulous sums of money actually to pay for the privilege of being inserted into one of these 200 mph accidents apparently just looking for a place to happen? Jonathan Palmer's answer is simple: 'The first thing for me – and this may come as a surprise in view of everything else I've said – is that I do actually love driving cars quickly. I'm a big kid, really, when it

Injured at Spa in 1985, Palmer spent much of the winter strengthening his leg muscles

comes to the pure fun of driving. If I go out on the road I'll drive bloody quickly for the sheer exhilaration of taking something – in this case, the control of driving – to an absolute limit.'

What happens when that limit is reached? How can a driver face with equanimity the prospect of losing that control – and with it his life? The answer – as far as Palmer and a number of others are concerned – is not to think about it. He should know: in the 1985 World Endurance Championship season Palmer himself survived a huge accident while driving a Porsche at Spa, and was fortunate to escape the fate of West German Grand Prix stars Manfred Winkelhock and Stefan Bellof, both killed within a few weeks of each other in endurance-racing crashes. 'I've been subjected to a big accident,' says Palmer, who spent much of the winter of 1984–5 rebuilding leg muscles as a result, 'and I haven't gone away saying I'm not going to go racing again because it's too quick. Motor racing is always going to be dangerous. What's probably more important than controlling speeds alone is the relationship between safety and speed. A driver, I believe, can control a car if it's doing 350 mph on a straight or 250 mph round the corners. We're *miles* off the limit of what the human body can control.'

No one would know better than Nigel Mansell just what those limits are – and not just in physical terms. Consider what the Midlander calls 'the lowest ebb of my career'. It was 1978, and he had sold his house – with the blessing of his wife Rosanne, both are quick to point out – to finance his racing. He had also given up a good job with Lucas Aerospace to concentrate on the sport. Then in a Formula Three race at Brands Hatch Mansell somersaulted, broke his neck, and could have been left a quadriplegic.

Throwback: John Surtees, here in a Ferrari at Monza in 1964, had ambition enough to win a world championship and go on to build his own cars

Surtees' title was sandwiched between the championship years of Jim Clark, 1963 and 1965

Within weeks he was back in the cockpit. The next year ended with another accident – and badly crushed vertebrae. But keeping the injury a secret, Mansell accepted an offer to test-drive a Formula One Lotus for Colin Chapman. He impressed, was taken on, and made his début in Austria at the Österreichring Grand Prix in 1980. It was only after the race that it was discovered he had driven sitting in a bath of fuel. A leak from the petrol tank resulted in first- and second-degree burns – and a hero's tag from the world's press.

But Mansell, it has to be said, is not always the easiest of drivers to get on with. His single-minded determination, no different from the best of the rest, makes him suffer those whom he considers to be fools very lightly indeed. He freely admits his best friend on the race circuits – and off them – is his wife, and Rosanne echoes his thoughts: 'We probably don't have friends in the business, more acquaintances,' she says. 'I mean, it's nice to see everybody. We enjoy the beginning of a new season, it's like going back to school. But whether you really class them as close friends I don't know.'

On this particular subject – that of being more than a nodding acquaintance of those with whom you work, or paradoxically, in the case of the Grand Prix driver, against whom you work – France's Jacques Laffite bemoans the passing of the years when a friend *was* a friend. Laffite is the most senior of Grand Prix veterans. His career, begun in Germany in 1974, included 167 Grands Prix to the end of 1985, taking in four teams and two lengthy spells with the Ligier outfit from his native France. In 1986 he was set to become the longest-serving Formula One driver of all: he needed four Grands Prix to equal Niki Lauda's total of 171, and ten to overhaul Graham Hill, long ensconced on the top of the drivers' list as the man with most races to his credit. Riccardo Patrese of Italy was the nearest of the current drivers, but almost 40 Grands Prix behind 'Jolly Jacques'. Surely no one is better qualified to comment on the state of the present Formula One world and the demands it makes of a driver?

In a *Motor Sport* interview in 1983, Laffite was already putting some distance between himself and the set-up as it now seems to him: 'I love the racing as much as ever, but the political aspect of the business is something which irritates me. When I first started racing in 1974 we used to practise, race, then have a walk round the paddock and chat with everybody. Now there's no time for that sort of thing. If I'm not at a team debriefing, then I might be at a GPRDA[1] meeting or at a meeting with FISA.[2]' A certain tiredness comes through those words, but Laffite, one of the most popular figures in any paddock, was quick to balance that with his feelings about his peers. 'But when we're out there in our cars on a Sunday afternoon,' he

[1] Grand Prix Racing Drivers' Association.
[2] Fédération Internationale du Sport Automobile.

went on, 'then is the time that I really enjoy myself. I'm strapped into my car, away from all the irrelevant problems, and you are aware that a degree of sportsmanship still exists within this increasingly professional business.' There, in a nutshell, is the difference between the Grand Prix driver and those of us who can only stand and admire: his problems actually evaporate when he is behind the wheel . . .

But back to the British and to Mansell. Friends or not, hang-ups or not, there was no disputing the genuine feeling of warmth and affection for Nigel at a certain Kent track last year as the leaves began to turn. 'If fairy tales were written about motor racing, there couldn't have been a better tale written for a British driver.'

Nigel Mansell, of course, talking after his first Grand Prix victory at the Grand Prix of Europe in front of his home crowd at Brands Hatch in October 1985. 'Everybody was absolutely fantastic. There was uncontrollable joy. Men and women alike were crying. It was a very emotional time. I don't remember crying since being a small boy but I certainly had a tear in my eye. I had a lot of emotion in me.'

It was Mansell's seventy-second race in a Grand Prix career which had started a little over five years before at that Austrian Grand Prix, driving for his then mentor Colin Chapman. After Chapman's death in December 1983 an unhappy period at Lotus followed, until his 'transfer' to Williams at the start of 1985. Under the dynamic Frank Williams, Mansell blossomed:

April 1985	Portugal, fifth
May	San Marino, fifth
	Monaco, front row of grid
June	Canada, sixth
	Detroit, front row of grid
August	Germany, sixth
	Austria, front row of grid
	Holland, sixth
	Italy, fastest lap
September	Belgium, second
October	Europe, first
	South Africa, pole position and first
November	Australia, front row of grid

Although the year ended on a flat note for Mansell, forced out of the Adelaide race on the first lap after a 'coming together' with Ayrton Senna, he says he bears no grudges – even though he was going for a third consecutive win. 'I got a very good start off the line, but what people didn't realise was my gearbox had exploded. It was quite frightening – me in the lead,

Opposite above, *Mansell's 1985 breakthrough at Brands*; below, *A well-earned thumbs up*

twenty-five cars behind me and I was thinking the transmission was going to seize up any minute.

'I decided I must get through those few turns on to the straight and pull over. Coming out of the third turn I applied the throttle more tentatively because of the vibration. Ayrton thought this was his chance and came alongside forgetting that at the next left-hander it is only possible for one car to go through. One can't blame him for taking the opportunity but I was out of the race already.

'Had there been nothing wrong with my car, there would have been no opening for him in the first place. If he had come through then I would have closed the door and taken both of us out I expect. I suppose it did add insult to injury, though, because if Senna had thought about it he would have realised there was something wrong with my car and he would have been through anyway.'

There is, however, no love lost between the two men. After all, Senna not only took Mansell's place at Lotus when the team felt Mansell was no longer good enough for them, but the Brazilian also tried to push Mansell off, according to Mansell himself, at Brands Hatch before his famous victory. The feud, for that is what it seems to be to some commentators, continued at the start of the 1986 season with the two again tangling, and again on the first lap, in Brazil. Out went Nigel, and this time he was said to be very angry. He had wanted to win for Frank Williams, by now lying paralysed in a hospital bed after a horrific road accident in France. Consolation for Nigel and the team was that Nelson Piquet won for Williams, forcing the 'old

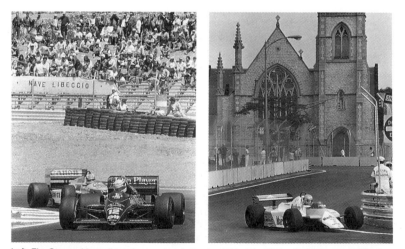

Left, *The Senna–Mansell tussle raged on in Spain;* right, *John Watson's McLaren at Detroit*

enemy' Senna into second place. Consolation, too, from an unexpected source – rival team boss Ken Tyrrell: 'The team that beats Williams in 1986 will be the team that wins the championship,' says Ken. The rivalry would continue, with a closely-fought duel in the second Grand Prix of the season, in Spain, which Senna won from Mansell by just 93 centimetres!

There is little point in asking any Grand Prix driver what it is that motivates him. There is only one goal – the world title. For most Formula One drivers it is an obsession and Mansell is no exception. If he has turned the corner and is poised for greatness, it is not without the same struggle that fellow countryman Jonathan Palmer has had – and perhaps, in a less than competitive team, is still having.

For Palmer, at least, the waters were – at first – unclouded by the existence of a second driver in the team to contend with. As the remarkable goings-on in the Lotus camp at the start of the 1986 season demonstrated, the choice of drivers to work together as teammates in the hothouse atmosphere of Grand Prix racing calls for diplomacy, or courage, or simply a thick skin on the part of the man who makes the decision. When the No. 1 driver is as clearly established as Ayrton Senna in the Hethel team, the role of No. 2 is a thankless one, to say the least. Hence the praise heaped upon Johnny Dumfries, for taking on the challenge in the first place, and responding with such fine opening drives in Rio and Jerez.

The internal problems that prevented Britain's Derek Warwick from joining the Lotus team as No. 2 to Senna could be seen, with differences of degree, in many other Formula One camps in the winter of 1985–6. On the

Dumfries at speed on the splendid Imola circuit in 1986

one hand there are the interesting personality clashes among the super-stars of the Grand Prix firmament: Prost and Rosberg at McLaren, Piquet and Mansell at Williams, Laffite and Arnoux in France's revitalised Ligier team. On the other hand there is the struggle for recognition among drivers still completing the transition to Formula One: Philippe Streiff, the likeable Frenchman from Grenoble, had to swallow some pride and accept second place to Britain's Martin Brundle in the Tyrrell team, with not-quite-equal treatment in the equipment pecking order, especially when the team's new challenger, the 015, was launched. Make no mistake about it, the first enemy, when you drive in a two-car team, is the man in the other car with your colours.

Until the arrival of Huub Rothengatter, Palmer counted himself lucky to be the solo star of the West German West-Zakspeed set-up: 'I preferred to be the solitary member, because we were at a stage where there was a lot of development to be done,' was his comment in the close season after his first year with Erich Zakowski's team. 'I certainly wouldn't say that my directions were better than anybody else's, but I do have a lot of confidence in my abilities in that area, and it's much simpler for a team to have direction coming just one way.' This left Palmer free to concentrate on whatever he could come up with in the effort to help his engineers improve the physical make-up of his car, quite apart from giving him the peace to get on with his own driving and honing those particular skills to perfection. 'Each driver explains things in a different way,' he maintains, 'and for the team it can be difficult to know quite who to react to. With me as the only driver there was no internal conflict or difference of opinion that could cloud the issue. I did recognise, however, that a 'faster' teammate might make me go faster too!'

An eight-month season of unrelenting effort, then, with the strain of travel from London to the great cities of the world, be they Rio, Adelaide, Johannesburg or Mexico City. But there is a close season, however short. How do the drivers occupy that time, and do they ever get away from it all? The highly-organised Palmer has one set of answers to those questions, mostly looking forward to the start of the following season: 'What I'm asking myself', he mused in the gloom of an English winter, 'is what I can do to improve my results. It's selfish, I admit that. I want to do well for me, and as a secondary thing for Zakspeed.' One way of improving performance was to draw up a checklist in triplicate, each time a test session is finished, detailing changes needed. A copy for the driver, one for the team manager, and one for the chief mechanic responsible for having the changes carried out: that way no one can escape the charge if work demanded is not done.

Meticulous note-taker though he is, Palmer does not neglect the practical side of his work: 'I'll also be doing a fair bit of testing,' he added, 'in France and Germany, with weekly visits to Germany until the beginning of the new

Palmer's graduation to Zakspeed came in 1985 and continued (top left) *into the new season*

season. I'll also be recruiting a few personal sponsors, organising how I'm going to look after them, and reviewing the public relations situation.' You can just see the attaché-case tucked somewhere under the dashboard of that pretty little Zakspeed! Joking apart, the excellent doctor also insisted he would be having a week's holiday in the close season of 1985–6 – the first in something like five years, which only goes to show how much effort goes into the drive towards that glamorous-looking place on the Rio grid.

Speaking of holidays, other drivers take the proverbial busman's. Tyrrell's Martin Brundle, for example, started the 1986 Formula One season with the avowed intention of having his first crack at the Lombard RAC Rally in November, a couple of weeks after the end of the Grand Prix round – something not many of the modern breed have done in an increasingly specialised sport. The Norfolk youngster is bringing back fond memories for a number of motor-sport fans who recall the days when someone like Jim Clark would take the exquisite skills he showed on the circuit out into the inhospitable forests and moorlands of Britain in a rallying winter.

Nigel Mansell, perhaps predictably, wintered in his Isle of Man tax-haven home. He has spent what one can only imagine is a small fortune on his hilltop 'complex' above picturesque Port Erin, making the kind of home for his wife and children that he never had as a youngster. He's blasted a new, and private, drive up the hillside, with the obligatory electronic gates; he's built a helicopter landing pad to accommodate the chopper he is learning to

Vaulting ambition? No – learning to fly makes Mansell's globe-trotting much easier

fly and in which he has bought 100 hours of flying time. 'Using a helicopter when I'm in England on business saves an enormous amount of time.' He has also built a snooker room in the basement of the house, but his pride and joy is at the bottom of the garden – or really at the top, bearing in mind which way the hill goes! Up there is a large swimming pool, jaccuzzi, running machine, weights – you name it, Mansell has got it. And just off the sumptuous indoor surroundings, kept at a constant 85°F – 'just like the Rio temperature' – there is a fully-furnished sitting-room with patio windows, overlooking everything that he has worked for. It is to this room that he comes after every race. The 'unwinding' there takes three days – away from everyone and everything, especially the telephone.

'The Isle of Man really is a world on its own. It's not an escape so much, as a better way of life than that on offer in England. It's safe for the children [daughter Cloe and son Leo]. We don't have to worry about muggings and rapes. In fact for the last three months on the south of the island we've had zero crime. We don't have traffic congestion, and there aren't the social worries of bringing up a family here that exist on the mainland. That's not shirking responsibilities because obviously we have them. The children travel the world with us, but I feel that from a family and an environmental point of view, if one's got the choice of living in a place like this or living a more hectic life-style, I'd pick this every time.'

To return to the original question then. Why do they do it? The money,

Senna's first win, Portugal, 1985

Legends to aim at: Lauda (left) and Stewart

undoubtedly, is good: men like Niki Lauda and Keke Rosberg don't fly Lear jets if their racing activities are unrewarding. But there would be hard work ahead for anyone trying to find out just how good the money is! Was there ever a sport more secretive about the sums of money it takes to oil its innumerable wheels? The speed itself is heart-pumping, the danger an ever-present stimulus to the flow of adrenalin through the human frame. But basically it all boils down to achievement. 'The second point', said Jonathan Palmer, after describing the sheer joy of driving fast, 'is that I'm an intensely competitive individual, and I really am only happy when I'm being success-ful at something. I'm a dreadful loser at anything. I'm terribly ambitious as well. In a way I wish I was of a different make-up: I wish I was the sort of person who could be satisfied and enjoy living without needing so much success.'

Put so succinctly, driving ambition is perfectly easy to understand. It is the basic human instinct of wanting to do something better than the next man can. As John Watson has said, the fact that a racing driver does it in combination with the most complex assembly of man-made machinery merely adds to the constantly repeated challenge of dragging the best out of himself. Armed with that knowledge, we may now ask how driving ambition is put into practice, bearing in mind Rex Hays' words: 'It is surely true that even the most brilliantly designed automobile – whether it is for racing or shopping – is but a heap of bits and pieces until brought to life by that even more remarkable mechanism, the human being.'

CHAPTER THREE
PRACTICE MAKES PERFECT...

The press box is not usually the most demonstrative section of any sporting crowd. For one thing, the assembled scribes are too busy trying to meet deadlines or showing their fabled objectivity, to get carried away by the events at which they are privileged spectators. For another, sporting journalists are just about the most cynical bunch of individuals you could hope to come across! But now and again they show a human face; they too are caught up in the sheer excitement that sport can generate, when a great team, or player, or competitor, does something unique and provides the familiar electric charge we all seek from our private vantage-point.

Such a moment came at Silverstone in 1985, and when it did it had the hardened hacks in the press box on their feet in the way a stunning goal at the Cup Final would. In that moment were encapsulated not only the brilliance of a racing driver but also all the puzzling questions about the way in which Grand Prix teams practise, prepare and qualify for any given race.

The competitor in question was 1982 world champion Keke Rosberg, then at the wheel of a Williams–Honda. It was the Saturday of British Grand Prix weekend – a weekend that showed the other side of Grand Prix racing with a vengeance. Leaden skies, torrents of rain, the former airfield windswept and bleak as the gathering faithful huddled under canvas. They needed a break, something to lift the gloom: in the afternoon they got it in the shape of one of the greatest laps we are ever likely to see on any Grand Prix circuit anywhere. Flying Finn Rosberg, also known as Rocky to his admirers, illuminated the whole season by becoming the first man to break the 160 mph barrier at one of the fastest tracks in the Grand Prix world. That average speed gave him pole position with a time of 1 minute 05.591 seconds, the fastest lap ever recorded in Grand Prix qualifying.

What the record books do not show is Rosberg flinging the blue, white and yellow Williams into that Woodcote chicane and fighting to hold it at the end of a lap made more difficult by rain out in the country and the fact that he had to get past two slower cars in a single manoeuvre. They do not show, either, how that one moment transformed a grey English afternoon into a golden memory that thousands of onlookers will not quickly forget. 'That looked exciting,' commented one of the aforementioned hacks to Rosberg at the subsequent press conference. 'At 160 mph it's pretty exciting from where I sit,' was the typical Finnish response.

Silverstone, 1985: British Grand Prix qualifying star Keke Rosberg waits to go out

But the very flippancy of the replay draws a discreet veil over one of the deep-seated problems posed by the qualifying system as it currently operates: the fact that drivers are given so little margin for error as they compete for those all-important places near the front of the grid at circuits where the job of overtaking under racing conditions can be pretty well impossible. The previous chapter asked 'Why do they do it?' This one might well follow up by asking why they do it in such a funny way.

What practice is all about is establishing the order in which the cars will start any given race. To begin with, how many cars can take part? A maximum of twenty-six, with the exception of glamorous Monaco. There the narrow streets – or is it all those double-parked yachts? – make it inadvisable for more than twenty to be unleashed on the Monegasque public. To qualify for the grid, the cars – a maximum of thirty, or twenty-six at Monaco – are subjected to a series of practice sessions in which their aims are twofold: firstly, to achieve a minimum qualifying standard outside which they will not be allowed to compete (DNQ – Did Not Qualify – is the most depressing mnemonic in the sport); and secondly, to achieve the very best time they can and thus be as far forward as possible when the cars line up two by two, for the start of the serious action.

A Grand Prix, therefore, is a thing of three days rather than one; and with three full days required on the circuit itself that means, in effect, that the teams must be there on the Thursday to start practice bright and early on Friday morning, while the earliest they can hope to head for home is late on the Sunday evening, or more probably early Monday. Add to that the sheer time-wasting involved in modern air travel and you have an idea of the chunk taken out of the fortnightly cycle.

Practice, then, takes place on the Friday and Saturday ahead of each race (three days before, where Monaco is concerned), and is further subdivided into untimed and timed sessions. Untimed, that is, in the official sense: but even those sessions are the subject of careful chronometry by the teams themselves, as they assess various facets of their cars' performance prior to the effort of actually getting into the race. The untimed sessions run from 10.00 to 11.30 on the Friday and Saturday: the interval between each of those and the timed session must not be less than ninety minutes. If anything happens to interrupt a session there is a knock-on effect, whereby the lost time is added on at the end (rather like a referee stopping his watch during an incident on the field). This can be exasperating for teams and drivers, and downright infuriating for the members of the press who see their deadlines approaching more rapidly than a 1200 bhp Formula One machine!

Silverstone start, 1985: Senna leads Rosberg, Prost and Piquet

In case you were wondering, things most certainly do happen. In the unhappiest circumstances, a driver involved in an accident during practice must be freed from his car and given whatever treatment is necessary, and the circuit must be cleared of debris. Sometimes the weather is to blame: in 1985 at Silverstone the cloud cover on the Friday was so low that the medical services' helicopter was unable to get in; without it the drivers are not allowed to go out on the track, so the early session had to be delayed. On other occasions the grounds for delay have been rather more colourful, to say the least. Take Rio at the start of the 1986 season, for example: a case of local law gone haywire held up the first untimed session for what seemed an unconscionable time, but was aggravated by the fact that turbo fires on two cars had already been the cause of one hold-up. The full story on that second break never quite emerged, but it seemed that the Brazilian boys in blue, peeved at not being allocated enough race tickets (for whom?), decided to take the law even more firmly into their own hands and close the circuit: no cars in or out of the pit lane, which made for a period of blessed if rather strained silence. The upshot: FISA slapped a $50,000 fine on the race organisers and threatened to take away their toys (in this case, the 1987 Brazilian Grand Prix) if they did not promise not to behave like that again.

Testing time: René Arnoux finds the Rio pace hotting up in February 1986

Three weeks later in Spain the first practice session was delayed for ninety minutes while the course marshals were stuck at the main gate because they had not been issued with the right passes.

Back to the serious business. The difference between untimed and timed practice is dramatic, not only because the element of competition is missing from the former, but also because of the rules that govern the latter. 'Anything goes' may not quite describe the untimed practice sessions, but teams do use them for a variety of purposes: checking times on full or empty tanks – very important when fuel capacity has been reduced to only 195 litres; assessing the performance of various tyre compounds, or mixtures of tyres between left and right, front and rear (if a circuit has nine right-hand turns and only three left-handers, it stands to reason that wear on left tyres will be greater than on the right under the strain of cornering); making any adjustments the driver may call for in the mechanical set-up of the car, or its aerodynamic balance; any experiments with engine-boost pressures; or simply getting a new driver acclimatised to a new circuit. Any lessons learned on the Friday will be incorporated into the car's make-up for the start of the Saturday untimed session – unless, of course, the team decide just to change things anyway and see what happens! But the

Life can be hard in the pits – especially when BRM is being beaten by Ferrari in 1952

untimed practices are very much a classroom for all involved – driver, engineer, mechanics and team manager are all anxious to extract the maximum of information from those ninety minutes because of their vital bearing on the timed sessions.

These afternoon periods are entirely different. The object now is to do what racing cars and their drivers are made for: to go round a circuit as quickly as the two together can manage. But this new, competitive game has its own inviolable set of rules. For a start, no one driver may use more than eight tyres, no matter how many cars he drives (his own, his team-mate's in an emergency, or the spare car if the team can stretch to one). The only exception to this rule is in wet weather, when there is no restriction on the use of treaded tyres on a wet track (a decision made, by the way, by the Clerk of the Course and the race organisers). Normally, thirty minutes before the start of each official practice session each competitor has in his pit the eight tyres for each of his drivers. Each of these tyres is marked by marshals on its outer face (driver's number, and letter characterising the race in question). A different colour is used to make these marks for each timed session.

The tyre limit and the performance of qualifying rubber also contribute to another key factor in timed practice: each driver has only two shots at setting a qualifying time. These are the so-called 'flying laps', which have been the subject of heated debate among motor-racing fans in recent years. Given that a set of tyres must be run for a little while to warm up to the temperature at which they perform to maximum effect – holding a 200 mph missile on the road – and that the tyres used in qualifying 'go off', or lose their grip, very rapidly, the driver must get out on the track, bed in the tyres, cross the line for his flying lap and then use a further lap as deceleration before returning to his pit. It may seem miserly, but it makes for some interesting moments, not infrequently to do with what Grand Prix drivers disarmingly call 'traffic' – slower cars on the circuit, either building up to or winding down from their own flying laps, that baulk another car attempting to set a qualifying time. This traffic has been the cause of some of the more impassioned conversations between drivers in recent years . . .

In theory, a driver out to set a qualifying time is competing, in the first instance, against two elements: the circuit, whose every curve, incline and idiosyncrasy he must know by heart; and himself – can he find the drive within himself to shave another few hundredths of a second off what looked like a decent first flying lap but has been surpassed by one of the opposition? For in practice one eye at least is always on the drivers under the other twenty-five helmets. The crucial point about qualifying is that it is a competi-

Opposite, Helmets have to be got right too – in this case for Messrs Mansell and Rosberg

tion within a competition, a separate trial of strength before the entry of the gladiators on the Sunday afternoon. This, and the fact that some cars on the circuit will of necessity be going so much faster than others at any given time in the session, has led to charges that the current qualifying system is downright dangerous.

One man who does not subscribe to that theory is Jonathan Palmer. 'I don't know that qualifying is as bad as all that,' he reflects. 'There are some things about it that are ridiculous, but it's a complex issue. To many people – teams, sponsors or spectators – qualifying is regarded as a completely separate aspect of a Grand Prix weekend. All right, the grid will affect the outcome of the race to a certain extent, but it's limited, so the value of qualifying is far more for the prestige of pole position, or for the image that being a midfield runner rather than a tail-end Charlie gives you. People within the sport tend to attach more importance to where a car qualifies than to where it eventually finishes.'

What help can a driver call on in his bid to win this separate little dust-up? Rubber, for a start: as we have seen, the compound used for qualifying is ultra-sticky, designed to give a very few laps of super-glue adhesion and help put down on the road the power the modern engine can provide. And here we have the nub of the whole affair: engines. For there are such things as special qualifying engines: colourfully described by John Watson as 'hand-grenades', these are special units wound up to a limit of internal

Plenty to keep an eye on for Alboreto and Johansson in a 1986 Ferrari cockpit

'So I did it this way': new boy Dumfries entertains double world champion Nelson Piquet

tension that will perform for a flying lap, under the constant threat of disintegration into so much costly shrapnel. Not all teams enjoy this privilege – with engines costing in excess of $40,000, who can afford them? – and there is the key to a debate given more point by proposed FISA changes for 1987. Immediately after the Rio race in 1986, an editorial in *Autosport* returned to the perennial problems of qualifying: cost and risk. In fact, of the thirteen constructors involved at the start of the new season, eleven voted for a change to qualifying procedures, only to be blocked by the other two under the ruling that insists on unanimity before change can be introduced. As *Autosport* so correctly pointed out, teams these days are no longer turbo or non-turbo, but 'rich' or 'poor'. 'The "I'm all right, Jack" mentality of the major F1 teams was never stronger than now,' said one of motor racing's most widely-respected organs.

Not that the use of qualifying engines is necessarily an unmixed blessing. Back in 1984, for example, Nelson Piquet put his BMW-powered Brabham on the pole no fewer than nine times, but hardly finished a race. The fact that, when he did, he finished first only added more frustration to this two-sided experience. Speed is the essence of the qualifying engine: the reliability half of our familiar equation goes up in a puff of smoke, often almost literally. Ken Tyrrell has referred to the use of special engines for qualifying as 'a ridiculous situation' and added that if he wielded power he would stipulate the use of a pop-off valve, at least in practice. This little gadget, widely used in North American racing, plays a similar role to the more familiar rev limiter. Working to a predetermined setting, it controls the boost pressure to the engine and literally pops off to prevent it being exceeded. But what alternatives to the current system could there be?

'Whatever happens,' opines Jonathan Palmer, 'a set of tyres is always going to be better when it's fresh. This is always going to be on the first couple of laps, so people will do their banzai laps on the second or third with that set of tyres – that won't change a great deal. On the engine side, people will obviously turn up the boost a great deal. The cars *are* a hell of a lot faster in qualifying than the race, and qualifying speeds have no real relevance to race speeds – but so what?'

What about allowing each driver out on to the circuit on his own, without the worry of coming across traffic? Given the time already spent in setting up for a Grand Prix, most people believe that an impractical burden on the hours available. As for setting predetermined speeds beyond which the cars should not be able to go, Palmer finds that equally unsatisfactory: 'The first issue in qualifying is: how fast do you want the cars to go? If you're going to start saying what's too fast, you've got to put figures on it, put it in terms of accceleration. For example, no car shall be able to accccelerate at a

Opposite, *No rest for the drivers in the good old days: Moss, as usual, looks in control*

rate greater than one G; the same for lateral acceleration – restrict cornering limits to two G. Now if you limit those, that gives you a ceiling lap-time, and maybe that's reasonable. But if you do that, you must then maintain the speeds of the other formulae, and I don't think that will ever happen.'

Given these reservations, it seems unlikely that major changes in qualifying procedure will come in the near future – especially if the big boys who can afford special qualifying engines refuse to play the same game as the little ones. For those of us who watch Grand Prix racing, therefore, the idea is to sit or stand back and watch the fun as the gallant twenty-six bid for that all-important pole position. Here is a genuinely separate competition: in a sport awash with statistics of all kinds, whether connected with drivers, races, circuits, engines or a hundred other aspects of Formula One, the number of pole positions per driver is one of the most keenly studied. Bear in mind that pole position often brings with it a nice little prize – at the British Grand Prix, for example, there is an engaging tradition of giving 100 bottles of best bubbly to the driver setting the fastest qualifying time, which must ease the pain of actually getting out there and doing it.

Thus it is interesting to note that, of the twenty-one world champions (some, of course, winners of the title more than once), only on seven occasions has anyone managed more than five pole positions in the year of taking the drivers' crown. The great Alberto Ascari of Italy was the first, six pole positions coming in only nine races in 1953, his second successive season as champion of the world. Next was Jim Clark, with seven in 1963 from a total of ten races, and two years later the Lotus ace did it again with six pole positions in ten starts. Jackie Stewart also took six from eleven in 1971, but the king of them all was the great Austrian Niki Lauda. In his fabulous 1975 world championship year for Ferrari, 'The Rat' left the pack trailing with no fewer than nine pole positions in his fourteen Grands Prix, winning five of the races to prove that speed and reliability were well and truly married. The following year James Hunt was on pole eight times, half of the season's sixteen races, on his way to the championship, but the last man to show such dominance was American all-rounder Mario Andretti, whose brief partnership with Colin Chapman's Lotus yielded eight pole positions and six chequered flags in 1978 as the team took both the drivers' and constructors' titles.

To return briefly to the sombre side of motor racing, and the number of drivers who have lost their lives since the death of Clark in 1968. It is distressing to note that some of our greatest Grand Prix heroes have perished in qualifying, from François Cévert in the USA, to Jochen Rindt at Monza in 1970, to the incomparable little Canadian, Gilles Villeneuve.

The record books show that pole position at Zolder on Sunday 9 May 1982 was occupied by the Renault of Alain Prost, then part of an all-French

Unqualified successes: top, Senna looks on in Portugal; bottom, Villeneuve in Spain in 1981

line-up with René Arnoux. Once again the facts behind the figures make for unpleasant reading. The race was run without Ferraris, the red cars whose presence seem always to have been a cornerstone of Grand Prix racing. To understand their absence we have to go back a further fortnight in time, to the race at Imola in which Ferrari's drivers, Villeneuve and Frenchman

Didier Pironi, suddenly became enemies on the track. Villeneuve was cruising to what would have been his seventh Grand Prix success, his teammate in tow as the Maranello stable headed for a one–two finish. But for reasons best known to himself, Pironi disregarded the team orders to slow down and conserve fuel, threw protocol to the winds, and snatched his own second win from under the Canadian's nose. An outraged Villeneuve swore never to speak to Pironi again, a sentiment that was to come true in a way he could never have anticipated.

When they got to Zolder, Villeneuve seemed determined to prove a point, and final qualifying on the Saturday afternoon seemed like the time to do it. Had he not just seen Pironi go out and better his own best lap-time by the merest hair's breadth? Villeneuve had one set of qualifying tyres left. Friday had gone up in a cloud of burning rubber when his flying lap was brought to a premature halt by a slowing car. So the darling of Grand Prix fans went out for his final lap in the seat of the Ferrari he had graced for almost five seasons. The same thing happened as the day before, and tragically for Jochen Mass it was again his March that got in the way of the flying Ferrari. With a left-hand turn approaching, Mass, aware that Villeneuve was rushing up behind, moved over to let the Canadian take the racing line. Villeneuve seems to have believed that Mass would stay exactly where he was, and flicked his own car right at that very moment. In an instant the Ferrari was catapulted into the air off the rear of the March, just like a launching-pad: the force flung Villeneuve across the circuit and through catch-fencing, inflict-

Testing time, again in Rio: Lauda and the McLaren team feeling the strain in 1985

ing injuries that claimed his life later that night. The second Ferrari was instantly withdrawn from the race as thousands mourned the loss of yet another friend. A distraught Pironi was to be the victim of a practice accident himself only three months later, after setting pole-position time for the German Grand Prix at Hockenheim; the damage to his legs has prevented his return to a racing car since.

The incident is the extreme case of those problems that the qualifying system creates. But if drivers themselves are not happy with the alternative suggestions, and if unanimity cannot prevail among the teams, what is to be done? Ultimately there is no way of making the sport safe – all that can be done is to restrict the arbitrary nature of the risks the drivers incur. Ironically enough, Villeneuve had first drawn attention to himself as a Formula One driver with a fine performance in qualifying on his first outing in a McLaren at Silverstone on British Grand Prix weekend in 1977. 'Villeneuve is a qualified sensation,' proclaimed *Motoring News* as it reported the Canadian's fine display: top in the two Wednesday sessions that saw him go through to timed practice proper and put the car on the fifth row of his first-ever Grand Prix grid. It was the kind of driving that made Villeneuve the last Grand Prix driver really to capture the hearts of *all* who watch the sport.

There is a final aspect of practice which we have ignored so far, yet it speaks volumes for – or against – the whole system we have been looking at. This is the 'race warm-up', conducted on race-day itself, but no less than four hours before the scheduled start of the actual race. This last, 30-minute period is once again a completely different story from the rest of the practice set-up: its purpose is to allow teams any final changes to their cars in the light of their performance in full racing trim. In theory, the time between its finish and the green light to start the race is enough to allow a complete engine change, though such extremes of circumstance are rare. More often than not, the race warm-up gives a radically different impression of what is about to happen than anything that qualifying may have thrown up.

As proof we need look only at the fortunes of the team that dominated Formula One in the seasons 1984 and 1985. In those two years McLarens, with TAG-Porsche power units, won no fewer than twelve Grands Prix and took other points on seventeen occasions. They took pole position, however, only five times, and then thanks only to Prost. Niki Lauda, the 1984 world champion who claimed six of those wins, was not once the pole-sitter: yet race-day warm-up was always the time when the McLarens seemed to say, 'This is when it matters: we may be starting from a little way back, but now watch what we can do in racing trim ...' And so, almost invariably, it would turn out. Disregarding the fashion of using special engines, McLaren simply concentrated on getting into the race, because they knew that when they did they would survive and usually surpass.

Lauda himself, one of the most astute and readable thinkers in the sport, makes no bones about qualifying, a system which he always scorned. In his marvellous book *Second Time Around* he talks about the last-minute choices made during warm-up, and goes on: 'My next step is to find out how fast I really am relative to my rivals. For this, the warm-up gives a much better indication than the pre-race qualifying runs on the previous days. In the first place, practically all the cars have put on race tyres and are fuelled for the race itself; in the second, the turbos are using normal boost pressure as opposed to the increased amount used for qualifying. Thus, for the first time in the whole weekend, I have a chance to see how my car is going to perform. The warm-up either bolsters your confidence for the race or leaves you with a frustrated feeling that it isn't going to be your day.' Enough said?

So, two days of practice, with two untimed sessions and two timed, all aimed at getting the final shape of a 26-car grid set up for the race; then a brief warm-up, moving closer to race conditions, a few hours before. Surely this is all the preparation needed before the thing gets under way in earnest? Well, yes and no. Yes, because there is nothing more teams or drivers can do to improve their lot before mechanical mayhem is unleashed when the green light goes on. No, because there are two more minor hurdles to get over before the unique sound of those massed engines reverberates across the plains of France, the fields of England or the waters of the harbour at Monaco. One is the solitary warm-up lap; the other is that apparently straightforward but often shambolic moment we call the start.

What, you cry: another warm-up? Afraid so: this is the one that climaxes the countdown procedure before any Grand Prix can begin, rather in the same way as a space launch is carefully counted down to the moment of lift-off. Half an hour before the start the cars cruise out of the pit road and assume their positions on the grid. This may sound simple, but have you seen a modern Grand Prix grid on your television screen? Some of them bear more resemblance to Oxford Street on a busy Saturday than a race-track on a Formula One Sunday should. On the way round the drivers cast a last anxious eye over the mechanical side of things and worry about last-minute noises or twitches from their cars. Once on the grid, they will get out of the cockpit again – wouldn't you, if it were 35° Celsius and someone offered you a parasol? Minimum distance between the rows of the grid is seven metres; if two cars have set identical times, the one which did so first is given priority. Access to the grid closes five minutes before the time announced for the start: any car not there in time starts from the back of the grid or from the pit road. Similarly, the exit from the pit road has been closed fifteen minutes before the start: any car marooned in the pits may start only after the field has passed the pits exit on the first racing lap.

Once the drivers are back on board, a series of boards are displayed – at

Getting the message: Alboreto (left) and Senna listen carefully

five minutes before the start to show countdown has begun; at three minutes, when everyone except the drivers, team members using external energy sources to get a car started and officials must leave; and one minute, when the blast of noise from twenty-six engines heralds the approaching start. At the 30-second mark a green flag is shown to release the cars on their final one-lap warm-up, which must be completed in starting order. Once that green flag has gone up no last-second change of car is allowed. A characteristic sight then is the whole field weaving and zig-zagging across the circuit as they trundle round for the start itself. This is the last preparatory act, warming the race rubber up to effective temperature while at the same time avoiding picking up too much dirt.

Next comes one of the great nerve-tingling moments in any sport: the cars gathered on the grid awaiting the red light, with twenty-six pairs of feet and hands poised for co-ordinated and simultaneous action. It is also one of the most potentially chaotic moments any sport can offer, and the catalogue of start-line 'shunts' in recent years bears witness to the difficulty of getting more than two dozen highly-strung machines and the men within them away cleanly on a 60-lap motor race. As Lauda says, most of the drivers find this moment 'incredibly hairy': they have to hold several hundred horse-power balanced on the clutch, itself built for only one or two such standing starts, keeping the engine revolutions as steady as possible while not letting the car move forward. Jumping the gun can incur a time penalty and

make a nonsense of a blistering drive in the race itself. When the red light goes on, first gear is engaged and there is a six- to ten-second nerve-jangling wait for the green light to replace it and release the field: mustn't stall, but mustn't wear out the clutch either. Once the green light glows, go for it – no time for fancy stuff here, just let those wheels spin until you transmit the power to the road.

If you think the wheels and the engine are moving fast, what about the driver's heart? Research has shown that at certain moments on a race-day the Grand Prix driver's heart is pumping at a peak rate of 200 beats per second; for long periods the rate can stay as high as 160. It is not only the engines that have sophisticated metering systems nowadays. The medical men have taken increasing interest in measuring the stresses imposed on the human frame and its control systems by the intensity of a Grand Prix. Why else do modern racing drivers subject themselves to rigorous pro-grammes of physical fitness? Everyone, as we all know, performs better when in good condition: how much more applicable is this to the driver's situation when the stress on nerves and physical resilience is taken into account. At Rio in 1986, for example, the two drivers in the Tyrrell team faced a small but by no means negligible problem: for both Martin Brundle and Philippe Streiff it was the first time they had sat in a racing car in earnest since the end of the previous season, and the first thing to remind them of it was the muscles of the neck and shoulders. In the first place, a racing helmet is a heavy brute; secondly, the gravity forces imposed on a circuit with long curves like Jacarepagua are such that the back and upper body suffer considerable discomfort. The only thing is to do what exercises are possible, and let the quick-fire succession of races in the new season force the body to build up its own protection anew. Otherwise, sit in the pits and have someone apply sympathetic massage. Moreover, Streiff is one of several drivers who have their own personal training and dietary consultant.

All these hurdles, then, have to be overcome before the driver can settle to the task of winning a Grand Prix. The feeling persists that nothing will ever quite sort out the complex ritual of qualifying, so we may as well finish where we began: with a scene from qualifying that gave further ammunition to those who would like the whole business to stay exactly as it is because of the sheer pleasure it can provide. The scene this time is not rain-swept Silverstone, but the sunnier setting of Rio de Janeiro at the first race of the 1986 season. This year's curtain-raiser was made even more special by the duelling of two local heroes, race favourites from the time first practice began. In the (predominantly) yellow, white and blue corner, the Williams–Honda of Nelson Piquet, twice world champion, at last prised

Preceding page: Senna has gone, Mansell and Piquet follow, and Prost is going wide in pursuit – Brands Hatch 1985

Old style: Gonzales (top) tells Ascari how it's done. New style: Senna in his element

away from Brabham, about to have his first race in the Patrick Head-designed FW11; in the black and gold corner, his compatriot Ayrton Senna in the Lotus 98T, a young man bent on world championship glory, seemingly at any price. A latter-day clash of the Titans, indeed: and from the off it was clear there would be no quarter asked or given.

On Friday it was Nelson who triumphed: a qualifying time of 1 minute 26.266 seconds pushed the Williams over the 130 mph average-speed barrier and kept the young pretender in check, as Senna concentrated on other aspects of his car's set-up. But Saturday was another day. For Piquet it brought no improvement, indeed quite the opposite when he uncharacteristically spun off ten minutes before the end of the final session and was left to nurse a strained thumb and damaged self-esteem, while Senna went in pursuit of greater things. Only Senna knew what he was capable of – though most of us had a fairly good idea. When Piquet went off for his little excursion into the Rio scenery, Senna had still not made his final assault on the eighth pole position of his short but glorious career. The session was duly interrupted, and when at last the Lotus nosed out on to the track for Senna's death-or-glory bid there was little more than a minute of qualifying time left.

The first question was: could he get the car round the 3.126 miles of Jacarepagua in time to start his flying lap before the chequered flag fell to signify the end of the session? Several thousand pairs of eyes, not only Brazilian but from every sector of a sizeable crowd and from every other pit, watched for the blur of black and gold to hit the finishing straight. No sooner had JPS Lotus 98T No. 12 crossed the line for its flying lap, it seemed, than the flag fluttered, but Senna was away on one of the most stunning laps we were likely to see. When it finished, precisely 1 minute 25.501 seconds later, he had captured the pole position, displaced his local rival, and written another heart-stopping chapter of what bids fair to be one of the most remarkable Formula One stories of all time.

The whole qualifying palaver – tyres, engine, boost, fuel load, driver attitude – that made the moment possible simultaneously made a mockery of race speeds that saw eventual winner Nelson Piquet manage a best racing lap down in the 1:33s. But who cared? In the emotional, colour-filled atmosphere of Rio, Ayrton Senna had danced to his own carnival tune – and for once the rest of us just loved the music. Perfect? Well, nearly.

CHAPTER FOUR

...BUT MONEY MAKES THE CARS GO ROUND

Once upon a time Formula One cars proudly displayed their international colours – British racing green, the Italian red of Ferrari, the orange of Holland, the blue of France. Then along came the big bad wolf – or was it the fairy godmother? – in the shape of Colin Chapman. The Lotus supremo was not just a pioneer on the track but off it as well. He was the first to realise that he could not fight the challenge of his Grand Prix competitors with the help only of the trade companies – Dunlop, Ferodo and so on. So he sat down and wrote a personal letter to 100 top British firms.

The first positive reply came from a tobacco company, and to the amazement of the media – and the horror of many purists – the 1968 season saw Graham Hill and Jim Clark in red and gold cars – as Gold Leaf Team Lotus. Thus the enterprising Chapman, so sadly missed these days following his fatal heart attack in December 1983, set the sponsorship bandwagon rolling – into what is now the multi-million, multi-coloured, high-speed marketplace that is motor racing today.

Comedian Jasper Carrott oversimplifies the pounds, shillings and pence of Formula One when he laments: 'It's an awful lot of money just to watch adverts flash past at 200 mph.' An easy joke, but as usual it contains some truth. And if it is impossible to get at the exact truth – for sponsors, marketing men, advertising executives and their publicity people are paranoid about what their competitors are up to – some educated guesswork and the odd crumb dropped from a sponsor's lips produce something not so very far off the mark.

Let us consider first the sponsorship of the *event* – the Grand Prix meeting. The car firm Mitsubishi, together with the Australian Government, funded the first Grand Prix of Australia at the back end of 1985. In autumn 1986 that national beverage of the outback, Fosters, financially liquefies the event. For years, in the United Kingdom, the tobacco giants – Marlboro at Silverstone and John Player at Brands Hatch – came up with the backing. This year the Kent track will have sponsorship for the very first time for a British Grand Prix from a British oil company – Shell Oils. Surprisingly, last year's Grand Prix of Europe, at the same venue with the same sponsor, was believed to have been the first Grand Prix ever backed by an oil company – curious really when you consider the long product involvement with the sport.

The sponsorship mix: the car – trail-blazing Gold Leaf, Graham Hill and Lotus, 1968; the event – Mitsubishi Grand Prix, Adelaide, 1985; the glamour – Tio Pepe girls, Jerez, 1986

The event sponsor keeps its guests and the media men happy with a pack of 'goodies'

It would be fair to estimate that a company such as Shell would have to pay an absolute minimum of £300,000 for a meeting – for what amounts to buying the title of the event and the placing of advertisements around the circuit. That may sound like an awful lot of money, but remember a 30-second commercial – like the Morris Minor Shell advertisement shot at Silverstone last year – costs up to £100,000 to make. And there is much more to the equation than meets the eye, as Dennis Keeping, Shell Oils General Manager, explains: 'In sponsoring an activity such as the British Grand Prix you are satisfying a lot of dimensions. You are satisfying exposure of your name and producing a very good basis for hospitality to clients and customers. You are identified in an arena where an oil company should be – the motor-racing business – and, as our research confirms, we are seen by the ordinary motorist to be natural bedfellows with such activities.'

A company like Shell would probably not spend much more than the same amount again – £300,000 – on all the extra sponsor activities connected with a Grand Prix – advertising, hospitality, and the rest of it – but it is generally accepted the the tobacco giants would spend up to four times as much – a grand total way in excess of £1 million and probably nearer £2 million!

But all those noughts are nothing compared with where the real money goes – in the sponsorship of a *team*. It will cost a front-running, two-car Grand Prix team a *starting* figure of somewhere between £5 million and £7½ million to be competitive for a year.

Unbelievable? Well, not when you consider the wages of top drivers, the pay packets of a back-up staff of 100 people, engines that blow up, turbos that burn up, and sixteen races to travel to around the world, as well as pre-season testing in faraway places – twice last winter in Brazil, for example, for those teams able to afford it. Imagine then the impact when, last year, a mega-rich single sponsor appeared on the scene with an apparently endless amount of money to spend.

The then management of the American conglomerate Beatrice, whose products include Samsonite, Avis and Playtex, decided it would put £50 million into its *own* team for an initial period of five years. American Carl Haas, so successful in running a motor-racing team in the USA, was to head up the team with former World Champion Alan Jones and Frenchman Patrick Tambay at the wheels. Teddy Mayer, the former boss of McLaren, together with designer Tyler Alexander, were to build and run the cars from a factory near Heathrow. In charge of the F1 project for Beatrice was Dick Stahler. As he travelled around the European Grand Prix circuit in 1985, prior to the team's non-championship début in Italy, Stahler was, not unnaturally, enthusiastic about his baby. He told everyone that Beatrice had spent £20 million on television advertising during the Los Angeles Olympics. As a result, 'seven out of every ten Americans now know who Beatrice are'. To have achieved the same awareness world-wide would have cost eight times as much. For less than three times – a mere £50 million – the company were to buy their way on to the screens of nearly 1250 million viewers a year for five years. A plausible argument indeed.

Then along came a new boss at Beatrice. He didn't like the motor-racing plans – or Mr Stahler's arguments. The deal fell through. Beatrice, now suddenly the 'girl of slender means' in the eyes of the motor-racing fraternity, would have only a limited sponsorship role with its team in 1986, in preparation for a complete withdrawal from the sport in 1987.

British sponsorship money is very hard to find. It is sad but true that Derek Warwick would have been driving for Ken Tyrrell this year had a British company joined with the American computer giant, Data General, as the team's sponsors. No one rose to the bait and along came Frenchman Philippe Streiff – not yet in the same class as Warwick, with only six Grands

Beatrice froze its Grand Prix venture – Patrick Tambay carries on testing in the snow

Prix and one third place compared with Derek's fifty-eight Grands Prix and twelve placings – but with a French sponsor.

Ken Tyrrell, who has had more sponsorship 'problems' than most, is philosophical about it all. 'I don't feel bitter about the situation. Motor sport, and Grand Prix racing especially, is a professional sport, and the first thing a team must do is go out and find a "sponsor". If it cannot find a sponsor it should look inwards to itself to find out why, and in particular, for a team like mine, why British companies are not more involved in Formula One than they are. I think the problem is that too few British firms market their products all over the world and they cannot therefore take advantage of the exposure that Grand Prix racing can offer.'

So if the Tyrrell Team was to 'look inwards to itself' to find its *own* problem, what would it discover? A principal factor emerges: 'In the last couple of years,' says Tyrrell, 'our problem has been that we haven't been able to acquire a turbo-charged engine. This made us less competitive and therefore less attractive to sponsors. The situation only changed in February 1985 when we did a deal with Renault, but even then, of course, the engines weren't available until the middle of the year. Had we had the engine earlier, it is my view that we would in fact have continued to have received the Benetton sponsorship after we won the Detroit race in 1983 [Michele Alboreto from Keke Rosberg with John Watson third]. Certainly they wouldn't have gone to Alfa if we had had a turbo-charged engine.

'In fact, we alongside Arrows were trying to get the BMW engine. When BMW chose to sell it to Arrows it meant that there was no other engine manufacturer that could supply us. We did try to get Brian Hart to supply us with an engine, but he was already committed to too many teams. Without a turbo-charged engine we weren't really competitive.'

Had Benetton continued to have been interested in Tyrrell, would they have wanted to buy out the team as they subsequently did with Toleman?

'I don't think I would have wanted that to happen,' says Tyrrell. Sadly for them, under the circumstances the decision to go to Alfa was, in retrospect, a dreadful mistake, because the team never scored a championship point. When Alfa pulled out of Formula One, and Toleman were in some difficulty, it probably became financially opportune for Benetton to buy Toleman. But that wouldn't have happened had the sponsor stayed with us.'

Ken is adamant about one thing, however. 'Sponsorship is the wrong word anyway. The word brings notions of someone helping somebody else to do something. Involvement for what we call a "sponsor" in Formula One is not about that. It's about selling space on a car which will generate exposure for the company. If a company wants to do it, it's for the exposure of their product and not because they want to help someone out.'

The lack of a competitive engine, then, is the single most important reason for Tyrrell's lack of sponsorship – according to Ken Tyrrell. But what about the drivers?

They are quite clearly placed in two camps. There are the drivers every team wants and will pay for – with the sponsor's money, of course; and there are those drivers the teams want more for the cash they will provide to drive for the team than for their ability. Unkind but true. Ken Tyrrell again: 'Our total budget for our first full year in Formula One [1970] was £80,000 – and of that £20,000 was paid to Jackie Stewart. It is probably true that the McLaren team pays their drivers [Prost and Rosberg] £2 million each per year. That's £4 million before you start to build a car, buy engines and go racing. So the calibre of the drivers has a big influence on the budget.'

Then just to top up those sorts of pay packets, the men, and very occasionally women, behind the wheel are usually allowed certain personal sponsors as well. One British driver is alleged to have half a dozen such deals, each worth six-figure sums! As motor-racing journalist Russell Bulgin says of Ayrton Senna: 'With Lotus Senna is allowed up to two personal sponsors on his black overalls in addition to those backers stipulated by the team. The Banco Nacional sash around his midriff and the logos dotting a lime-yellow helmet are reputed to add $1 million to a basic $200,000 John

Opposite above, At least there was a future for Beatrice unlike the chasing Renault; below, 'Listen to me, my boy. I know all about sponsors. You just drive.' Ken and Martin

Opposite, *There's no mistaking Fabi's car;* above, *Jackie Stewart the driver – now a businessman*

Player Special retainer. Had Senna signed with Toleman or McLaren three years ago, he would not have been able to make independent deals such as the one with Banco Nacional. He would have sacrificed a measure – a vital measure – of commercial freedom.'

At the other end of the scale are those mere mortals who have to buy themselves a drive. It's a 'Catch 22' situation for them. No money, no drive. No drive, no sponsorship. We've already heard how Nigel Mansell sold his home to go racing and how Jonathan Palmer borrowed £100,000. More fortunate would-be Grand Prix stars have rich fathers – or friends in high places. Jonathan Palmer: 'I had sufficient ability and value to the Zakspeed team by 1985 for them to employ – and pay – me, even though they themselves were starting from scratch. So this year I am now established as a Grand Prix driver who's being paid, which is as important as the fact that I'm a driver who doesn't have to bring money into a team any more.'

The one thing that no sponsor wants is bad publicity, although there is a school of thought that any exposure *is* publicity. That was not the case for WD & HO Wills in 1968. Gold Leaf's obvious joy at being associated with Lotus and Graham Hill's World Championship must have been tempered by the death of Hill's Lotus teammate, Jim Clark. Admittedly Clark's untimely departure from the motor-racing scene was not in Formula One, but there must have been a few uneasy boardroom meetings back at Gold Leaf's Bristol headquarters.

Above, *Clark with Hill in the pre-sponsorship sixties;* opposite, *Senna – a sponsor's dream?*

Ken Tyrrell again: 'Brushes with authority have been hurtful to me financially. Take our ban in 1984, for example. We weren't banned for reasons that were valid. Because people wanted to change the regulations and we wouldn't agree, they found a way of ensuring our vote wouldn't be valid.' How damaging that subsequent ban was to the company is difficult to assess. 'You wouldn't expect a potential sponsor to understand what really happened . . . so I imagine some people probably thought we were cheating, and that hurts . . . even now. As most sponsors in Formula One are being chased by a number of teams anyway, probably enough poison was put about to influence sponsors' decisions.'

Team Tyrrell was banned in 1984 because of alleged fuel irregularities, and although the team's drivers, including Martin Brundle, finished in the top six in several races, the results did not count. Subsequently Ken Tyrrell cleared his name in the law courts but the 1984 ban stood.

How depressing is it for the drivers not to have a fully sponsored team? 'It's *very* depressing,' says Tyrrell's number one driver, Martin Brundle,

'because now that we have one sponsor [Data General] I think a lot more people would be prepared to come in because they feel there's security with the team. But before we couldn't seem to get that first sponsor, so we couldn't put money into research and development to make the car a regular winner – and we couldn't get sponsors because we were not getting regular wins. That really is the "Catch 22" and is very frustrating.'

But Brundle, who scored his first *official* world championship points at the beginning of the 1986 season with a fifth place in the *old* car in Brazil, does not feel that he is with a second-best team, a team that hasn't quite got what it now takes to win world championship titles for either the driver or the team. 'No, I don't feel like that at all. We're talking about a team that has won the World Championship three times. OK, that's several years ago now, but the team has regularly won Grands Prix. Ken Tyrrell knows how to win Grands Prix. He's done it many times and he's got a very good team around him. We've got the potential but it's now a question of getting the money for research and development to bring that potential together. There's no doubting that the team has got the right qualities to win. We just need the right equipment.' A classic statement.

Brundle is equally honest about the never-to-be partnership with Derek Warwick. 'I would have been very happy to have Derek alongside me at Tyrrell. I am in a very different situation to that of Ayrton Senna who did not want Derek with him at Lotus. Ayrton is in a team that is ready to win the

Another expensive soaking: Prost and Mansell celebrate at Brands Hatch, 1985

World Championship this year. We won't be there from Day One. Senna wanted a totally undiluted effort from his team because he felt that he could win the World Championship in a Lotus if Lotus gave all their attention to him. But two heads are better than one as far as Tyrrell and I are concerned, so Derek Warwick and myself in the same team would have got the new car sorted out in two or three races, which would have been good from that point of view.'

What happens when television and the sponsor do not see eye to eye – which, through very careful negotiation, rarely happens? Those people putting up the money want maximum exposure, and they wouldn't be doing their job if they didn't strive to get it. Equally television producers must ensure the advertising is not distracting the viewer from the racing. The racing, after all, is the only valid reason that cameras are present. At one track prior to a Grand Prix one year an advertisement appeared on what the television producer claimed was the track surface. Not so, said the circuit management, who had taken money for the advertisement; it was on the run-off area. But the fact of the matter was that the offending legend had appeared after the producer's visit to the track not only to site his cameras but to check on advertising as well, and this particular slogan was very much in camera shot. In the end the advertisement was blacked out and honour was restored all round – because the blacked-out letters could still be read if the viewer concentrated on them and not the race!

Nigel flies the flag after his memorable first win, Shell Oils Grand Prix of Europe

What about the unfortunate situation that arose ten years ago? First of all the London Rubber Company decided it wanted to 'normalise the name' of one of its products – and thus in 1976 Alan Jones and Henri Pescarolo appeared in the Surtees Durex. Television did not think the sponsorship conformed to an agreement hammered out with the motor-racing authorities back in 1968. Indeed, it was felt that no one was adhering to the agreement, which stipulated 'size and prominence of commercial advertising on racing cars, with the object of ensuring that the cameras would not be obliged to concentrate on obtrusive advertising at the heart of the action'.

Even allowing for the fact that the shape of cars had altered since the 1968 agreement – the year, remember, when Gold Leaf burst on to the scene – it was felt that the amount of advertising was way in excess of what had been discussed all those years before. So before the Race of Champions in 1976 the motor-racing authorities were asked to return to the 1968 agreement. They did not, and the television plugs were pulled – and poor James Hunt's winning year received scant coverage. Now was that television's fault or that of the sponsor?

Today FOCA (the Formula One Constructors' Association) and the EBU (the European Broadcasting Union) – the organisation to which most major television companies in Europe belong – have an agreement over advertising which, by now, has been established as part of the sponsorship 'mix'. Amongst other things it has been agreed that:
– there shall be no advertising between the cameras and the action, nor on the surface of the race circuit;
– there shall be no advertisements higher than 1.5 metres, fluorescent in colour, luminous or rotating;
– there shall be no advertisement 'in sound' during the television transmissions nor any that infringe the national rules of the country where the race takes place (for example, in the UK tobacco advertising is not allowed but the sponsorship of the event is – as are existing permanent signs).
All of which is highly complicated and requires a great deal of co-operation between all parties concerned, especially when you, the viewer at home or the trackside spectator, only want to get on and enjoy watching the *sport*. But the fact is that, without the money from the advertisers and the sponsors and the support of television and its resources, the sport would not exist as we know it today.

One way or another some of the sponsors' money must find its way into what FOCA calls the Prize Fund. No one will let on what the fund is, but what is known is that it is divided into three parts: twenty per cent according to qualifying results; forty-five per cent according to race results; and the remaining thirty-five per cent to something FOCA calls 'fixed compensation'.

The brilliant and much missed Colin Chapman with one of his beloved Lotus cars

Great drivers, small rewards: Stirling Moss and Mike Hawthorn in the old pre-sponsorship days

Let us take qualifying first. At the end of two days of official practice the team in pole position picks up 2% of the prize fund, and so on down the grid to the team in twentieth position, which picks up just 0.4% (for 21st to 26th place there is nothing).

Race results are even more confusing (probably a team with a computer sponsor comes in handy here). The team in the lead at quarter-distance in the race picks up 1.02% of the prize money, and at the same stage it is possible for the twentieth-place car still to earn something – in this case 0.036%. The winning car collects 5.44%, the twentieth car to finish gets 0.192%. In all, there are eighty categories in which cars can earn less or more of that 45% allocated to race results. Assuming a 'prize fund' of, say, $1 million maximum and, say, $650,000 minimum, a team whose driver leads from start to finish would collect 8.5% of the total – a reasonable return even at the lower figure!

Finally, the 35% left over for 'fixed compensation' is divided into two equal parts. One part is distributed to the competitors in proportion to the number of World Championship points scored in the previous two half-seasons; the second part is distributed equally amongst the twenty fastest qualifiers in each race during the first half of the season, and to the top ten teams (or cars) in the previous two half-seasons.

All very confusing, but very important to the teams consuming pound notes and dollar bills as if money was going out of fashion. But where will it go from this financial quagmire? No one can say, of course. Many bemoan the passing of the days when a driver leapt from his car at the end of a race and barbecued at the side of the track with his mechanics and spectators. Today there are sponsors' guests to meet, sponsors' gifts to hand out, sponsors' dinners to attend, and tomorrow a test session in another country, made possible, of course, with sponsors' money – and a little help from the prize fund!

It is not all that bad, though. The money is making the privileged few in motor racing very rich indeed, and if it wasn't for motor-racing sponsorship who would hear of Simod shoes or Samai trucks in Saudi Arabia, or Denim aftershave or De Longhi heaters in the Dominican Republic!

Colin Chapman loved it all. The helicopter flights to the circuits, the stately home in which to house his beloved Lotus team. His vision, nearly twenty years ago, set the ball rolling and, in the case of Lotus, started the longest-running sponsorship in the history of motor racing – one that has seen the John Player Special cars and Team Lotus celebrate four drivers' championships and five constructors' championships. Perhaps the team is on the verge of adding to that tally.

MAJOR SPONSORS 1986

McLaren International	Marlboro	tobacco
	Shell	petroleum
	Boss	clothing
	SAIMA	trucking
Data General Team Tyrrell	Data General	computers
	Elf	petroleum
Williams Grand Prix Engineering	Canon	cameras
	Honda	motor manufacturer
	Mobil	petroleum
	ICI	fibres
Brabham	Olivetti	computers
	Pirelli	tyres
Ram Automotive	Spirit of Australia	Australian businessmen
John Player Special Team Lotus	John Player Special	tobacco
	De Longhi	heaters
	Reporter	clothing
	Elf	petroleum
West Zakspeed	West	tobacco
Team Haas USA	Beatrice	multi-national
Barclay Arrows	Barclay	tobacco
	USF & G	finance
Benetton Formula	Benetton	clothing
	Sisley	clothing
Osella Squadra Corse	Kelemata	perfume
Minardi Team	Simod	shoes
Equipe Ligier Gitanes	Gitanes	tobacco
	Elf	petroleum
	Loto	football pools
Sefac Ferrari	Fiat	motor manufacturer
	Agip	petroleum
	Marlboro	tobacco
	Digital computers	computers

CHAPTER FIVE

IS MOTOR RACING THE PITS?

A certain tennis player may have made the expression fashionable as a synonym for all that is worst in the world, but motor racing really is the pits – that area at any circuit where the mechanics work in mysterious ways their wonders to perform. If the term suggests the bulk of this activity is pursued underground, the impression is correct: that is exactly how it came into use, though it has long outlived its origins. Soon after the French got this Grand Prix business going they realised there was a basic design flaw in their circuits, such as they were in 1908 or thereabouts when the pits came into being: it was a nuisance for the paying public to have to get from the outside of the track to the inside, where the grandstands were situated. So Dieppe decided to move them to the outside. It followed that, for the customers' view of cars at close quarters to remain unimpaired, these 'replenishment depots' had to be sunk below ground level. Try saying 'Here's Martin Brundle coming in for a quick replenishment depot stop' and you will understand why the unlovely name 'pits' became so popular . . .

Any Grand Prix watcher, even the most casual, will have been thrilled by the spectacle of a whole crew of mechanics swooping on a car almost before it has stopped to remove and replace four tyres, force in a new tankful of fuel, or repair a damaged part – all under the pressure of the stopwatch, perhaps when the driver is leading his race and desperate to get back out before the second man catches him. In the early eighties in particular, pit stops made for one of the most exciting features of Grand Prix racing, particularly when television viewers could see the hundredths of a second ticking by on their screens as the team went to work. Fears for safety, when gallons of highly inflammable fuel were being forced in under high pressure, and a number of near-serious accidents, put an end to that particular practice, but pit stops for tyres – depending on the rigours of a particular circuit – or for running repairs are still part of any Grand Prix.

Race theatricals apart, the pits focus our attention on refinements that nowadays threaten to take Grand Prix racing beyond the pale where many fireside fans are concerned. Given the pace of development in engine technology and chassis work, are we in danger of submersion by a welter of terms that mean little to the average viewer, or for that matter to a number of people intimately connected with the world of Formula One? World champion Alain Prost rejoices in the nickname of 'The Professor': sometimes it

Opposite, *Brundle says chocks away;* above, *Legendary manager Neubauer oversees a Donington pit stop*

seems a Masters in Science is a prerequisite for the modern racing driver who no longer has only a steering wheel, a set of pedals and levers and the odd corner to worry about, but is surrounded in his cramped cockpit by the most sophisticated engine telemetry, the occasional on-board cameras, and a permanent in-board computer to boot. With anti-roll bars, monocoques, turbochargers and all, the Formula One car of today is not so much a racer as a laboratory in high-speed motion.

And yet . . . It all boils down to the men who actually work in the pits: the machine has not been invented that can listen to an incoming driver, diagnose the problem he is reporting and set about correcting it, without human intervention. Some of these men are scientists in their own right, or graduates with top-class engineering qualifications; others are the team bosses who have a lifetime's experience of 'hands-on' involvement to draw on; but the bulk of them are mechanics whose job is the least glamorous but the most crucial of all.

In general terms, each driver will have his own crew, specially designated to look after his car. This will consist of a race engineer and two or possibly three mechanics, depending on the resources an individual team can call upon. To take an average-sized set-up, the Data General Team Tyrrell race contingent at the start of the 1986 season numbered fourteen or so: two mechanics per car and two general mechanics – one of them an electrician; chief mechanic and chief engineer; three others with specific duties such as looking after tyres, spares or general fetching and carrying; and add to that chief designer Maurice Phillippe and team manager Ken Tyrrell himself. The emphasis is very much on teamwork: the coordination of every man's efforts in order to maximise the potential of the team as a whole and make life less difficult for the most isolated member of the whole crew, the driver in his cockpit.

To lessen his isolation, the latter – again in the more well-to-do outfits – is blessed (or is it cursed?) by the presence in his helmet of a radio linking him with the pits. Thus, if something goes wrong on the far side of a typical circuit, he can signal ahead to his pit that he will be coming in next time round. Stories about these marvels of modern communication abound, not least of the well-known driver of a French persuasion who used his radio to sing 'Happy Birthday' to his bewildered team manager. More often than not, however, the link-up consists of a plug-in jack that fits the driver's helmet and is immediately attached when he pulls into the pit area. Without it, the noise of a Grand Prix pit lane would prevent much practical exchange of information, and so it is that a typical pit area these days looks like a pop convention, with grown men walking around with larger-than-usual personal stereos on their heads.

Engine specialists, radio links, a photographer here and there: crowded pit lane at Imola

Tyrrell team at work: a camera keeps an eye on Streiff (top), Bellof lends an ear

What the television viewer sees is at best the full racing span of his home Grand Prix: this takes in a little of the warm-up procedure, some scene-setting and the post-race celebrations. All of this adds up to something less than three hours of admittedly intense activity for the driver and sometimes exhausting emotion for the spectator. What it does not reflect is the man-hours the average mechanic puts in. They are invariably the first people to arrive at the circuit and just as invariably the last to leave – unless team performance has been so short-lived they can make an early getaway while the others have yet to pack up. From morning till night they are engaged in high-speed work at the sharp end, for on their efforts may depend the chances of a driver's success: get it wrong on a Grand Prix car and the consequences are not to be thought about . . .

The point is that they rarely do get it wrong. Each aspect of the pit crew's work is rehearsed until it is down to a fine art; each movement planned for maximum economy of effort; every inch of available space used as purposefully as it can be. These modern garages are the equivalent of an operating theatre, the surgery that goes on there every bit as delicate as the repair work carried out on an anatomy only marginally more complex. Instead of scalpels and scissors, airguns and spanners are neatly laid out on work benches as meticulously organised as a doctor's tray. While one man is dissecting the innards of a gearbox, another is finishing off the livery of the car with adhesive numbers or good old-fashioned paint; as one wheels in a trolley of fresh tyres, his partner carries out a nose cone for repainting or an aerofoil for minor modifications. Behind the team's pits area is its transporter, a kind of mobile spare-parts centre that not only carries the cars but plays home to items as diverse as team souvenirs and timing devices.

Nowadays much of the human effort – on the lighter side of the pit activity – can be taken care of by electronic systems: each team, for example, has at its disposal a screen or screens, usually mounted on the wall that divides the pit lane from the actual track, giving lap-by-lap information on race positions, speeds, lap times, the gap between first, second and the rest, and so on. Such is the sophistication of present-day timing that at Brands Hatch, for example, a digital 'clock' on the control tower flashes up the speed any particular car is achieving as it crosses a sensitised line on the circuit. All round the track teams of observers with the latest in measurement wizardry are stationed with walkie-talkie radios: they sit at machines which look for all the world like a rather large tape recorder or recording console lined with buttons saying 'Arm 1' or 'Trigger 2', their purpose being not to fire at the passing cars but to monitor speeds at a given point. These are instantly printed out on the machine and read off by one of the two operators via radio link to a central point in the race control-tower. From

Opposite, *Pit lane scene: Mansell's Williams at Silverstone for the British Grand Prix in 1985*

there a complete set of race statistics, or practice times, is compiled and printed out in great numbers for the interested parties, including the several hundred members of the world's press in attendance at every Grand Prix on a crowded international calendar.

What used to be a chore for a team member standing by the pit wall, stopwatch in hand, is now the sort of technology that can analyse for us the closest possible racing finish, and do so in seconds. Remember the inaugural Grand Prix on the brand-new circuit at Jerez, Spain? That was the day when a pit stop more or less cost Nigel Mansell his third Grand Prix win for Williams and safeguarded Ayrton Senna's own third success with Lotus. The Manx driver led with only ten laps of the seventy-two left but was frustrated by a puncture to a rear tyre. Circumstances conspired to stop him coming in for a change of rubber when the team wanted him to; and when eventually Mansell did come in his crew achieved the minor miracle of getting him back out again in 8.7 seconds. But so close was that Spanish race that even this was not enough to keep the Williams in front. Past went the Lotus, past went the McLaren of reigning world champion Alain Prost, and Mansell was held up for almost a lap before he could get past the Frenchman and have Senna in his sights again. As the two raced for the line, Mansell ate into the gap until he was on the Brazilian's tail with one lap left. By the time they negotiated the hairpin leading to Jerez's short finishing straight, the Williams was pulling alongside its rival; as they crossed the line the naked eye saw little more than a flash of colour and knew only that Mansell was in front by the turn into the corner after the pits. Thanks to modern timing skills it was possible to put a figure on the closest Grand Prix finish for fifteen years and say that Senna held on by fourteen thousandths of a second – a gap that represents little more than ninety-three centimetres at the speeds these machines can reach. Even the drivers weren't quite sure who had won.

If gadgetry is now established outside the pits, it is also taking over one of the most important functions within: the setting-up of a modern engine to cope with the various demands a different circuit, or a change of weather, or a change of Formula One regulations, will impose. What do you do, for example, when the maximum fuel load available to any car in any Grand Prix is 220 litres at the end of one season and drops to 195 by the start of the next? The answer lies in computers: engine-management systems are used nowadays to implement changes in the power unit's workings that govern fuel consumption, oil and water temperatures, and a host of other variables the computer can adjust to more rapidly than the mere human

Heart-stopping pit-stopping: opposite above, Senna's Lotus gets the treatment. below, What a tangled web these engine-makers – in this case Renault – weave

intelligence. It can take up to an hour to fire up a modern racing engine: as well as the crew of mechanics and engineers belonging to each team, a familiar sight in any pit area are the technicians working on behalf of the engine manufacturer, whose job it is to consult established data, program an in-board computer accordingly, and respond to the new data it provides in the course of practice or racing sessions. This is diagnostic work at its most subtle, and it is fair to say that the pace of development in engine technology in the last decade is the single most remarkable feature of the progress of Formula One.

Surgery of a kind, we called it, and doctors are commonly seen as people with superior brainpower. Why not call on Dr Palmer again to give his view of how this breathless evolution affects the driver? What degree of technical know-how is required before a man climbs into a Grand Prix cockpit nowadays? 'There isn't a defined level of technical expertise that's needed; you have great drivers with very limited technical ability, and you can have, to be honest, quite mediocre drivers who are virtually engineers. So the technical ability of a driver is just another variable that gets thrown into the package. However, I firmly believe that – assuming all other values are equal – a driver with more technical knowledge will do better for himself and the team than one without, just because the way you are going to go faster is ninety per cent down to improving the car. There's still ten per cent or so

Villeneuve in Spain, 1981: the split in his Ferrari number shows the 'skirt' at work

that comes from the driver, I believe, but if a driver is more technically-minded and can help improve that other ninety per cent then he can find himself half a second or a second per lap quite easily.'

As usual, Palmer has his finger on the pulse; and as usual the root of the question lies in the money being poured into Grand Prix racing. 'The cars are more sophisticated than ever,' he adds, 'it's as simple as that. Overall, we've probably lost a bit of chassis sophistication compared to the "ground effect" days, when drivers had to be technically more sensitive to the aerodynamics because you could find or lose two or three seconds quite easily if the aerodynamics weren't quite right.'

What Palmer refers to here is the period in Formula One history in the late seventies and early eighties when cars were made to go more quickly simply because they were made to adhere more firmly to the tarmac. This 'ground effect' was the brainchild of Colin Chapman, starting with his designs for the Lotus 78 and 79. Put crudely, ground effect depends on the use of 'skirts' attached to the sides of the car, and intended to create a vacuum underneath it which increases the downforce exerted upon it, and thus almost literally pushes it down on to the track. It was not uncommon to hear the expression 'cornering on rails' as the results of this ground effect made it possible for Formula One cars to negotiate turns at speeds previously thought impossible without the most extreme consequences for

Renault threw money into their F1 effort, but it ended in an Adelaide farewell in 1985

Stripped for action: Prost waits for his McLaren to be dressed again

lateral stability. The underbody of the car was so shaped as to describe a curve rather than the traditional flat bottom, the aim being to induce 'negative lift', in direct contrast, as it were, to the design of an aeroplane wing and its function of raising the machinery off the ground.

It was this Chapman-inspired revolution that took Grand Prix racing-car design into the world of aviation science and made aerodynamics – the physics of gases in motion and their mechanical effects – the key to success. Hence the modern concern with wind-tunnel testing and the lessons it can teach on a car's ability to hold the road and the benefits to be derived from apparently the most minor modifications. At the speeds a car can reach in Formula One today, the flow of air over its various surfaces is a crucial factor in its handling characteristics; in the ground-effect era it was also the source of unparalleled discomfort for drivers as their bodies were exposed to hitherto unknown cornering conditions. As three-times world champion Niki Lauda so colourfully said, '"Cornering" was a euphemism for the out-and-out rape practised on the driver, the car and the laws of physics.' The forces exerted on the human anatomy by a Grand Prix car taking corners at the speeds permitted by ground-effect aerodynamics were such that the driver's head would be forced sideways and down in a process repeated corner after corner, lap upon lap, for a period of two hours or more: no wonder it was one of the least regretted changes in Formula One when, after 1982, flat bottoms became the order of the day again and skirts were no longer allowed – and all without a lady in sight . . .

If, as Jonathan Palmer has claimed, some of this 'sophistication' in aerodynamic design has been forsaken, the other principal area of racing-car development – the bit that puts the power in – has taken centre stage in a way Renault could scarcely have dreamed of when they launched the Grand Prix world upon the turbo path in the late seventies. The effect was to galvanise other manufacturers, with the happy result for the sport that at the start of the 1986 season there were no fewer than nine engine makes represented on the Grand Prix starting grids. 'Aerodynamics', insists Palmer, 'was a team's responsibility, i.e. there would be a hundred or so people at a major Formula One set-up like Williams or McLaren spending the bulk of their time on that particular area. Nowadays you've still got those 100, but you've also got the might of BMW, Honda, Porsche or Ford also trying to make the cars go faster by improving their engines.'

Putting it another way, 'the real purpose of racing is not to produce super-drivers but super-engineers'. So said Louis Delage, and he should know: as we saw in the first chapter, his French cars conquered the world in those early years of Grand Prix racing, not least of all at Brooklands when British spectators were left wondering at the gulf between the home product and the European invaders. What was true in the twenties holds good today: the engineering that goes into the Formula One car adapts the most advanced techniques and materials to the construction of missiles whose potential speeds seem virtually limitless. Those two hours on a Sunday when Murray Walker and his opposite numbers from other countries describe a race are only the tip of the Grand Prix iceberg. For a glimpse of what lies below the surface – water, this time, not the underground pits this chapter began with – a visit to a racing team's headquarters is a must.

As you might expect from a company that ties such gigantic names as Canon and Honda into its corporate identity, the Williams Grand Prix Engineering facility – note the deliberate thrust of the firm's name – at Didcot is a mighty impressive place. Opened in July 1984 by then Secretary of State for Defence Michael Heseltine, the plant occupies 39,000 square feet of purpose-built offices and shop-floor. It houses ninety-five people, from public relations staff to design engineers, secretaries to accountants. Among its enviable installations are a quarter-scale wind tunnel, an auto-clave – for baking the carbon-fibre moulded monocoque of the Grand Prix car – and an engine development laboratory built in conjunction with Williams' Japanese supplier, Honda.

The shop-floor is carefully divided into areas designated for specific purposes, with bays for each of the cars being worked on, and an astonishing amount of space for the crews to work in. Compare this with the back-street garage days of early motor racing and you have the clearest possible evidence that we are no longer dealing with a sport but with a high-tech industry only one of whose goals is the presentation of two racing cars on a fortnightly Grand Prix grid. 'We have the sort of guys who would have built Spitfires,' says the Williams press officer. 'They have an amazing amount of aggression and dedication to the job. They work up to seventeen hours a day – this is an industry different from any other.' As you look around and see in one corner the remains of two Grand Prix cars pranged in recent accidents, in another the shells of two new ones under construction, and catch fleeting glimpses of Oriental gentlemen slipping secretively through to their engine test-beds, you begin to have an inkling of what he means . . .

Through another door and it's into the wind-tunnel section. The machine is computer-programmed in such a way that the rolling road inside matches road speed to air speed and the design staff can simulate airflow through a car's radiators, into front brakes, its effects on the car's road-holding capacity – virtually all that is needed to let the designer either cry 'Eureka!' or go, literally, back to the drawing-board. The results speak for themselves: by the end of the 1985 season Honda had their engine sorted so that it was no longer simply a straight-line speed merchant but also built in that other essential half of the equation, reliability in racing conditions. That plus the

Above, *Arnoux hares out of the pits after a Ferrari pit stop in Montreal, 1983;* left, *A drinking tube is often essential to help drivers (in this case Senna) cope with cockpit temperatures*

that Williams Grand Prix Engineering facility is the most humble and by no means the most visible. It is a precise instrument of measurement, though not calibrated in hundredths of an inch or in millimetres, mph or any other precise unit. Be that as it may, it holds the key to that most important indicator of how any team is faring – its morale. For the scientific marvel attached to a wall of the Williams workshop is a common-or-garden frustration meter. Looking rather like an old school bell, it has four main readings – 'Getting on OK'; 'Normal'; 'Danger'; and 'Gone Home!'. Thus it turns its back on the mechanical side of this sometimes faceless sport and reminds us that, like any other human activity, it runs the gamut of emotions for the men who, in many people's eyes, matter most in Formula One: the backroom boys, and the mechanics in particular. Have you ever stopped to consider just how many possibilities of failure – how many degrees on the frustration meter – those 1500 pieces of metal, carbon fibre, rubber or other synthetic material on the Grand Prix car represent? No wonder the mechanics are famed for their sense of humour: without it they simply would not survive.

Which is why the most enjoyable moments of a Grand Prix weekend are often not those during the race itself. There is a time on the evening after a race when all the crowds have gone home, the sideshows have fallen quiet, the world's press are busy in their telex rooms or telephone cabins, and the Formula One paddock is a marvellous place in which to walk around. All you see is the mechanics still at work, stripping down engines, stowing away gear, packing up boxes, clearing out garages, tidying up pits, making sure they take away with them all the essential items of equipment they brought in the first place; and all the time exchanging gossip with the team next door, passing judgment on the race just finished, lamenting the unhappy lot a mechanic's lot always seems . . . In short, putting back the human face on the mechanised mayhem of the Grand Prix scene. Mind you, the job can often impose intolerable strains: if your driver has a shunt and you're a long way from home, the pressure of getting cars back to base for repair work means there is virtually no time to unwind at all. A two-day haul back to, say, England from the south of Spain or France; intense activity back at the factory to make and install any damaged parts, or to prepare cars for testing after an accident; and almost at once the need to get them back on the transporter and off to the Channel port in time for the next trip into Europe or further afield. This is the other, less glamorous face of Grand Prix racing, when the chips are down and a complex job has to be done in the tightest of schedules – and almost invariably it is. At home, as on the circuit, the mechanics are always first in, last out: small wonder that so many of them command the respect and gratitude of their drivers, or that their brief periods of leisure generate moments that pass into motor-racing mythology. The pits? All human life is there . . .

CHAPTER SIX

IN AND ON THE BOX

If not exactly the George Michael and Andrew Ridgeley of television sport, they are now as inseparable as Simon Le Bon and his yacht – or, in motor-racing parlance, slicks and dry-weather. They are, of course, Murray Walker and James Hunt. Murray is the son of Graham Walker, one of motor-cycle racing's British champions. Father and son became BBC television's motor-sports commentary team after Murray made his first broadcast in 1949. That partnership continued until Graham Walker's death in 1962. Nearly twenty years were to pass until, in 1981, Murray was joined by a new partner – former Formula One World Champion James Hunt.

James, unbelievably forty years old in August 1987, is the son of a stockbroker, the veteran of ninety-two Grands Prix between his début in a March for Lord Hesketh at Monaco in 1973 and his retirement in a Wolf, also at Monaco, in 1979. In those six years James also drove in Hesketh's own car and for McLaren, with whom he won the world title in 1976. Always making the headlines for one reason or another 'Hunt the Shunt', as he was affectionately known, crammed fourteen pole positions, ten victories and a host of memories into his all too short racing career.

He's married to Sarah, his second wife, and lives with her and son Tom in Wimbledon. His laid-back delivery at the microphone, coupled with his intimate knowledge of the sport and often cutting comments on current drivers, is the perfect foil for Murray's distinctive, excitable descriptions which British, and all English-speaking, motor-racing fans worldwide have come to expect from the former advertising executive.

Murray, now no longer addicted to motorbikes – until recently he owned a 900 cc and a 1000 cc BMW, lives with his wife Elizabeth in a small Hampshire village halfway between Bournemouth and Salisbury. And it's Murray who tells us why his practice 'nearly makes perfect . . .'

'I don't know how many Grands Prix I've seen. Hundreds, I suppose. My father was a professional Grand Prix motorcycle racer and I spent my childhood watching him compete in the Isle of Man TT and on the Continent. In fact it was because of that that I'm lucky enough to have seen the fabulous pre-war (World War Two, that is, he said hastily!) Mercedes Benz and Auto Unions in action.'

'"Do you still like it?" people ask me. Of course I do! The prospect of going to any Grand Prix still gives me a thrill of anticipation – a thrill which turns into four days of very real pleasure at each event. And a thrill which climaxes on Grand Prix Sunday when the green light comes on!

'But if there is a low point, especially at a race abroad, it's the post-race interview which goes like this: I've been at the circuit since very early in the morning, I've gradually built up, through the race-day preliminaries, to a state of anticipatory tension which has exploded into some one and a half hours of concentrated commentary action – often in far from enviable surroundings. The race finishes, the job is done, and the adrenalin is all used up. I put the microphone down, weary but relieved. And it is then that I hear in my earphones, from London, the voice of the *Grand Prix* programme producer, Roger Moody. "Not a bad old race, Murray – it'll come together well for tonight's programme. But I need an interview with the winner – oh, and see if you can get Niki Lauda to talk about why he retired. And if you can get Senna's reaction to running out of fuel I'd like that too." Yes, Roger. Anything you say, Roger. It's just that I'm on the opposite side of the track from the drivers. The circuit, the paddock and everywhere else is now jam-packed solid with a fanatical crowd, all trying to get at the same people as me. And my magic pass no longer works.

'But, nothing daunted, it's elbows out. Push. Shove. "Excuse me – BBC Television – I must get through." And when I do I find that Lauda's already halfway home to Ibiza in his Learjet, Senna's gone to his hotel, and Piquet, the winner, is already surrounded five deep by the world's media. Never mind. Ruthlessly push through, wind up the vocal chords and bellow,

The commentary team: producer Roger Moody, Murray, lap charter Mike Doodson, James

Top, *'It looked like Keke, James.'* *'No, Murray, it was Nelson.'* Bottom, *Who'd be a commentator?*

"Nelson – it's Murray. We're live on *Grandstand* and they're interrupting the Men's Finals at Wimbledon for us – *now*!" And, bless him, he comes to the camera. Yes, I know it may not have been totally true, but all's fair in love and war and that was a pitched battle!

Portugal belonged to Niki in 1984. Murray got locked in the circuit

'Just as it was in Monaco in 1982. Riccardo Patrese had won and, after the usual mayhem and "that's your problem" beastliness, I'd got him to the interview position. There was a problem, though. The camera was on the other side of the road – down which an enormous transporter was slowly making its inexorable way to block us out from Grandstand in about thirty seconds! That was certainly the ultimate stimulus to getting it right first time, which happily we did. Almost as bad as trying to interview Ayrton Senna after his first historic Grand Prix win in Portugal last year. Since the interview-room arrangements the previous year (when I had to talk to the new World Champion, Niki Lauda, and the gloriously defeated Alain Prost in a small dark room occupied by some 350 other media men) had been impossible-to-dangerous, the new arrangement was to have the post-race activities in a large tent into which only Special Pass Holders would be allowed. But it had poured with rain all day and the tent was more than fully occupied with anybody and everybody before Senna even appeared. Which, in turn, led to more than a few lost tempers when the agitated media men arrived, en masse, with deadlines to meet. The result was that my interview was literally conducted in the middle of a multi-nation punch-up of flailing fists, flying feet, broken cameras and shouted international obscenities. Happy days!

'The Portuguese Grand Prix is one of the newer – and very welcome – World Championship races, and it has already generated more than its share of memories for me. When we first went there in 1984 we were amazed and delighted at how well everything had been done by a country which hadn't hosted a Grand Prix since 1960. An excellent circuit, good organisation, first-class television coverage, and a cheerful atmosphere of friendliness and willingness to help and learn. So, after the interviews in the Black Hole of Estoril had been done and we'd enjoyed the Championship victory celebrations, some hours later we happily went to leave the circuit. Only to find that whichever gate, whichever exit, whichever way out we tried, we were firmly locked in!

'Not to worry we thought. We'll walk round the circuit, get in the commentary box, out through the back and away. As we did so I spotted a chest-high wall and reckoned a good short cut would be to climb it, flip myself over the top, and drop down the other side into the car park. As I was about to do so I was amazed to see a ladder suddenly appear over the parapet, followed immediately by a beaming Portuguese fireman. The drop I'd been unknowingly about to make was about thirty feet! Our fireman friend politely escorted us down his ladder, saving us a good half-mile walk and me two broken legs. We gave him a BBC-TV Grand Prix pen and he was so pleased he almost offered us his ladder as a souvenir.

'Most Grand Prix meetings start for me on the Thursday before the race, when I travel out with the producer and the engineer, and, in passing, what a joy it is to have them with me! Most of the countries which cover Grands Prix just send a commentator, who not only has to do his own job but also somehow try to deal with all the administrative and technical complexities as well. Like trying to overcome the problem of lost satellite links between Rio and London! The BBC way means I can get on with what I'm supposed to be doing – finding out what is happening and telling people about it – without also trying to be a technical genius and a producer as well. And that's a great comfort!

'For instance, when we arrived at the Jarama circuit for the Spanish Grand Prix in 1981 (the fantastic year when Villeneuve won and 1.24 seconds covered the first five to finish!) I saw, with horror, that I had to commentate from a twelve-inch black and white monitor, positioned in broad sunlight. Slightly put out by this I made polite representations to Roger Moody, and to Dave Wharton, the engineer. The result was frenzied activity, phone calls back to London, and clandestine meetings between Dave and his Spanish TV colleagues. After the last practice on Saturday Roger sidled up to me and said, without even moving his lips, "I think we've cracked it, Murray, but if we can't solve it here we've got a man actually waiting in London to fly out a colour monitor." How right he was, for on race-day when I arrived at the long row of commentary boxes in the main Grandstand, it was to find that the BBC – and the BBC alone – had been provided by Spanish TV with a colour monitor so large that I could hardly get in the box with it. Not a popular move with the commentators from all the other countries with their mini monotone monitors, but he who strikes first strikes hardest . . . ! They still talk to me about it and ask how I was able to work the oracle. "Get the power of the BBC around you, chaps, and you're away!" I say.

'The BBC commentaries not only go to the UK but also, live, to Australia, Canada, and a large part of North America which can receive Canadian TV. So we're conscious of a big responsibility in telling millions of sports fans all over the world what is happening where we are. It is hard work but great fun – which usually starts on the plane out. For we travel whenever we can with the special flights which are arranged by the Formula One Constructors' Association. That means the whole plane is filled with Grand Prix people – team owners, team managers, sponsors, drivers, mechanics, media people, and representatives of the specialist suppliers of items like tyres, plugs, brakes, fuel and electrical systems.

'So you'll have Gordon Murray, the Brabham designer, next to you, Martin Brundle in the seat in front, Nigel Mansell across the aisle, Peter Warr

Opposite, *Murray Walker the reporter with Britain's Derek Warwick, now happily back in F1 racing*

of JPS Lotus nearby, and everyone else around. The Grand Prix world is a small and closely-knit one where everyone knows everyone else, so the plane out is a great place to start beavering for the latest on what's going on!

'Beavering is, for me, a process which goes on non-stop until the race begins. Walking the course to see if there are any changes from last year. Watching the Friday and Saturday practice sessions to study the lines and gear-change points, time the laps and observe the cars' behaviour. Finding out what different tyre constructions and tread compounds are available and likely to be used. And talking. To the mechanics about what happened in the last session. To the designers about what changes they've made to their cars since the last race – and why (not that they'll tell you very often). To the team owners about the latest developments and the ever-present Grand Prix politics. To the sponsors about how they're doing (and the ever-present Grand Prix politics). To the race officials about the administration (and the ever-present . . .). And, of course, most of all to the drivers about their problems and prospects.

'Hard work or a holiday? Well, it's both really. Hard work because behind all the pleasurable talking is the pressure of knowing that, on Sunday, it's down to you to talk knowledgeably, authoritatively and, hopefully, entertainingly about an event where it's your job to interpret the pictures to millions of people – most of whom would give their eye teeth to be where you are! And in a sport as fast moving as Grand Prix racing, where the situation changes from second to second, where the action spreads over a very large area and lasts for some one and a half hours, that pressure can be considerable.

'Sometimes the situation can change for totally unexpected reasons! In France, where the Grand Prix is held in July when the weather is predictably hot and dry, the commentators, with devastating French logic, are stuck out in the open on a patch of grass with, if we're lucky, some woven matting overhead to prevent sunstroke. "Why give them a box when they don't need it?" you can imagine the TV people saying. "The fresh air'll do them good!" But at Dijon in 1981 Nemesis struck, in the form of an almost frighteningly violent rainstorm which not only stopped the race but soaked the Commentary Corps, turned their notes into pulp, and totally shorted all the electrics. That was the day that Alain Prost in his Renault made himself the hero of France by excitingly beating John Watson when the race restarted. But in an atmosphere of total confusion about who'd actually won, it was only some very nimble work by the technicians that enabled a soaking and disorientated bunch of international commentators to tell the outside world – and even then we weren't totally sure! Last year, at the Paul Ricard

Opposite, 'Monaco ... frenetic racing through the streets where the jet set and the ordinary punters really do meet'

The 'tifosi' at Monza (top) can become extremely excitable. Perhaps they would benefit from a hosing down like the ones the Rio crowd receive (bottom) when the temperature soars

circuit, French TV avoided a repetition of this problem by putting us all in a hermetically-sealed, non-air-conditioned Portacabin in a temperature of over 100 degrees!

'Ah well, I suppose you can't win them all, and what could be better than travelling the world at the centre of something you're passionately enthusiastic about? I'm certainly not complaining! Every circuit and country has its own distinctive atmosphere, which makes an ever-changing pattern of fascination, interest and excitement. Monaco, frenetic racing-through-the-streets where, although it's a hideous cliché, the jet-set and the ordinary punters really do meet and mingle under the sun amidst the yachts, the Lamborghinis, the five-star hotels and the topless beaches. Austria, for my money one of the finest circuits of them all, where the drivers twist, turn and swoop their way round the gloriously scenic Österreichring at breathtaking speed, and where half the crowd seems to be blind drunk! Monza, where racing history and tradition ooze from every inch of the track – the only circuit still in use where the immortals like Caracciola, Rosemeyer, Nuvolari and Varzi used to race before the war. And where the ambiance created by well over 100,000 fanatical Ferrari-loving "tifosi" is almost frightening in its intensity. Rio de Janeiro, where another raving, chanting 100,000-plus crowd is crammed into one gigantic granstand, and where it gets so hot that the City fire brigade regularly hoses them down! Watkins Glen in Upper New York State, where the hooliganism made the worst football crowd look like a Sunday nature ramble (like setting fire to spectators' cars and sinking them in the notorious "Bog", and literally dynamiting people's motorhomes. I've seen both happen!)

'But, at the other extreme, there's the pure unadulterated joy-of-occasion, superlative organisation, immaculate presentation and infectious enthusiasm that was Australia's first Grand Prix in Adelaide last year. Without doubt the most enjoyable and satisfying motor-sport event I've ever been to. And that's saying a lot!

'Put all that lot together and it massively overwhelms the dodgy bits. Even the obstructive officials (it is quite amazing how bloody-minded and unpleasant some people can be when they're put in charge of a gate). The ravening Alsatian guard-dogs at Dijon and Zeltweg. The delayed planes. The wrong passes. And the telephone problems. Because every minus seems to be cancelled by a plus. A couple of years ago after the Dutch Grand Prix, as we were wearily but happily about to return to our Amsterdam hotel, one of us who I suppose had better be nameless shut the car keys in the boot. Now I wasn't best pleased about this and was about to march grumpily off to the paddock to borrow a hammer to smash my way into our inoffensive Ford Sierra when the producer – for it was he who was the culprit – blandly appears with two large policemen. "What do you think they can do about it then?" I said. "Sir," said one (they all speak flawless English!), "we have a lot of experience with Sierras. Please allow us." So saying he took off his uniform cap and dismantled it to remove a stiffening wire with which, after two hours of patient work, he opened the door. "There Sir," he said, "and please enjoy the rest of your stay in Holland." I don't know that Ford would have liked it but we certainly did! And much as I admire our excellent police I wonder if two Dutch-speaking TV men would have fared as well in the same circumstances at Brands Hatch!

'As for my "partner", well . . . there are many stories about James we can tell in the next book, assuming of course his lawyers agree! For my part, I very much enjoy having him in the commentary "cockpit", even on the occasion when I spent the whole race with his plastered leg in my lap!

'Like it? I love it! It certainly is a great life and I can only hope that you enjoy listening to your BBC commentary team half as much as I, for my part, enjoy talking to you.'

CHAPTER SEVEN

'POSITIVE SCREENING'

Mick the drummer, John the guitarist and their backing singers – two Americans and one British – began it all again eight years ago. Another American with an Italian-sounding name wrapped it all up nine months later. 'It' was the return to television coverage of motor racing by the BBC. Together Mick Fleetwood and John McVie had given their names to 'Fleetwood Mac', the pop group with its roots in the Swinging Sixties whose emotive record 'Rumours' gave that fledgling programme *Grand Prix* its signature tune in May 1978.

The American with the foreign-sounding name? Mario Andretti – winner of six races and the World Drivers' Championship that year – the year when Bjorn Borg beat Jimmy Connors in the Men's final at Wimbledon and Argentina won the Football World Cup.

Motor-racing buffs will be quick to point out that Argentina, in January, saw the start of the Formula One season that year, not Monaco in May when the *Grand Prix* television programme began. The Buenos Aires race, where incidentally Andretti posted his intention of taking the crown by beating reigning world champion Niki Lauda into second place, found its way into *Sportsnight* – as did the USA West event from Long Beach three months later. There was no airing for either Brazil or South Africa, but where better to start than that Mediterranean jewel in the crown – Monte Carlo.

Andretti was already leading the championship in his Lotus, tying with Carlos Reutemann in the Ferrari on eighteen points; Lauda was still waiting for his first success of the year; and James Hunt – well, he hadn't finished in any of the three previous races! The winner was dark horse Patrick Depailler driving a Tyrrell. The viewing figures for that early summer's evening of Monaco highlights, on BBC2 at nearly 11 pm, were a respectable half-million – and that despite the fact that it was a new programme – and that the next day was a Monday!

By July, and the British Grand Prix at Brands Hatch, $2\frac{1}{2}$ million viewers watched Reutemann's victory. The trend continued. In 1985 the same venue hosted the Grand Prix of Europe, and the first-ever win for Britain's Nigel Mansell in his Williams. Nearly eight million BBC viewers watched the race 'live' on television in the afternoon or the recorded highlights in the evening, and around the world a staggering eighty million people tuned in to see the race either as it happened or in recorded form later.

Privateer Reg Parnell drove for five teams in six Grands Prix

But we are getting ahead of ourselves. Why did motor racing *return* to British television in 1978? When did it begin? How was it covered then and how is it done now? What part has television played in bringing the sport into public recognition? Would privateer Reg Parnell ever have dreamed of *live* pictures *from* his Maserati as he flew around the champagne cellars of Reims in 1950? Thirty-five years later nearly eighty million viewers would thrill to Patrick Tambay's attempts to produce something spectacular for Renault in their swansong in Adelaide – and every one of those viewers was in the cockpit in Australia with the Frenchman, albeit for just 6½ laps!

In one sense the television outside broadcast story begins, not at Brooklands or Aintree, or even Donington, but in the much more serene setting of Wimbledon. No, there never was a motor race there, but the BBC's first-ever outside broadcast came from the famous centre court, that mid-summer day of 1937 when Bunny Austin played George Rogers under the eagle eye of tennis commentator Freddie Grisewood. Sixteen years were to pass before an armchair audience was to witness the first-ever *live* pictures of a Grand Prix on television.

Silverstone was the setting; the date – 18 July 1953; reigning World Champion Ascari was about to win for Ferrari and Italy; the BBC's producer that day was John Vernon (later to switch to directing television coverage of the somewhat slower boat race!); a youthful Raymond Baxter was the commentator, aided and abetted by Robin Richards; John Cooper was the lap charter and technical advice came from W. H. Hartley.

As Raymond said then: 'With first-time television coverage of the meeting we hope to bring some of the thrills of the circuit to a wider audience than the tens of thousands of spectators who will flock to the meeting from every corner of the country. To the enthusiast there is no substitute for the battering roar of exhaust and that thrilling combination of hot oil, hot rubber and continental cigarette smoke which is the bouquet of speed. We hope to explain some of the apparent intricacies of the game and to introduce some of the personalities and machinery which make motor racing a sport and a spectacle unique in its appeal and character.'

Heady words, Raymond, but it worked. With just a minimum number of cameras (including one on the bridge looking back down the start/finish line), one and a half million viewers saw the race. As a gesture of appreciation the BBC made a 'donation' to the British Racing Drivers' Club!

The first post-war televising of Grand Prix motor racing had been at the 1949 Silverstone race, not then a World Championship event. Just why the broadcast took place many months later – in January 1950 – is not clear. Perhaps editing highlights took a little longer than the hours, sometimes minutes, that is the case today! For the record, that was the second Grand Prix at Silverstone, but the first to be given the name *British* Grand Prix. The

18 SATURDAY

Televis

10.0-11.0 app. **MOTOR RACING AT SILVERSTONE**

The fifth R.A.C. British Grand Prix Meeting, organised by the British Racing Drivers' Club in co-operation with the *Daily Express*

The 500 c.c. Race

Commentator : Raymond Baxter

who writes on page 43

★　　★　　★

2.45 RACING AT ASCOT

3.20 The King George VI and the Queen Elizabeth Stakes

Commentator, Peter Dimmock assisted by Peter O'Sullevan a race-reader

Clive Graham identifies the horse and jockeys from a position ove looking the Parade Ring

3.30　MOTOR RACING

at **Silverstone**

The fifth R.A.C. British Grand Prix Meeting

The International Sports Car Race

Commentator, Raymond Bax

3.50 RACING AT ASCOT

3.55 The Princess Margaret Stakes

Commentator, Peter O'Sull

Parade Ring Commentat Clive Graham

4.0　MOTOR RACING

Further commentaries f Silverstone

Commen Raymond Glende assisted by Tom E. Webste Parade Ring Commentator : Clive Graham

4.35 app. **MOTOR RACING**

Further commentaries from Silverstone

R A C Bro

The plan was to pilot a manned rocket some 1,50 observation purposes and then to return. The pro theory, but in practice . . . Nigel Kneale's ne

'The Quatermass Ex

n **Programmes**

ED OCTOBER 1, 1937

SATURDAY, October 9

2.25 ROAD RACE for the Imperial Trophy. The first International Road Race in London (by courtesy of the Road Racing Club), on the Crystal Palace Road Racing Circuit (conditions permitting)

EVISION *of the* WEEK

7 MAY 1978

5.51 FIRST TIME ERE. (Details as Tuesday, 9.15)

3.46 ROAD RACE. (See 2.25)

SUNDAY tv

10.50 Grand Prix
covering motor-racing's Formula One World Championship on Sundays through the summer, and featuring tonight:
The Monaco Grand Prix
The classic two-mile circuit round the houses of the fashionable Mediterranean principality is the first European venue of the championship. After four rounds so far, the honours are even between Colin Chapman's British Lotus team and the Italian Ferraris with two wins each. Lotus's MARIO ANDRETTI (US) and Ferrari's CARLOS REUTEMANN (Argentina) share the lead in the Drivers' Championship. The reigning champion NIKI LAUDA, twice a winner at Monaco, still waits for his first success of 1978, while JAMES HUNT will aim to improve on his record of not finishing in the last three races.
Leading positions:
M. Andretti (US) — Lotus   18
C. Reutemann (Arg) — Ferrari 18
R. Peterson (Swe) — Lotus   14
P. Depailler (Fra) — Tyrrell 14
N. Lauda (Austria) — Brabham 10
Commentator MURRAY WALKER

TV presentation by the
SOCIÉTÉ FRANÇAISE DE PRODUCTION
Editor JONATHAN MARTIN
(On 21 May: The Belgian Grand Prix)

AT SILVERSTC
This year

above the earth
d very reasonable
begins at 8.15

ment'

elevision Diary,' page

'CAFE
NTINENTAL
International Ca
h Hélène Cordet
tress of Ceremo
'Hôtel, Père Au
t your service
chestre Pigalle
d by Sydney Jerom
sed and produced
Henry Caldwell

CING AT ASCOT
erecording of som
ty's racing

TOR RACING
recording of som
ag at Silverstone

eather Forecast a
S (sound only)

course had been altered from the previous year, as Peter Carrick explained in his book, *Silverstone – the Story of Britain's Fastest Circuit*: 'The potentially dangerous U-turns were eliminated and the runway was not used, except for a slow chicane which had been constructed at Club Corner. A lap was now three miles, the 100 laps of the Grand Prix giving a distance of just 300 miles.' Incidentally, Baron Emanuel de Graffenried won in his Maserati and spectators paid 25/- for a 'pits grandstand seat'.

But back to television and to Crystal Palace of all places, where not only did the BBC have its South-East transmitter but from where the first-*ever* race to be covered by TV cameras was run. The event – it had to be the *Imperial* Trophy. The date – 9 October 1937. It was won by Prince Bira in an ERA. He completed the 15-lap race on the two-mile circuit at an average speed of 57.8 mph. Crystal Palace also ran motor races for the Imperial Plate and the Coronation Trophy and, according to the RAC, still may hold those trophies! You may well park on part of the old motor-racing track when you go there now to watch Steve Cram or Zola Budd.

One other 'first'. Thirty-four years after that Crystal Palace race the first *colour* television coverage of motor racing in the UK took place. We are back at Silverstone again and the date is 18 July 1971. Jackie Stewart took the flag that day on his way to his second World Championship title. It has to be admitted, however, that throughout the first quarter of a century of the Grand Prix World Championship television coverage was, to say the least, inevitably sketchy, and some *aficionados* will be quick to stress that the sport's heyday was not adequately covered by television worldwide.

That was all to change with the emergence of one man – sometime racing driver, one-time trainee chemist and all-time businessman, Bernie Ecclestone. The Formula One Constructors' Association (FOCA) had grown out of almost a 'drinking club' in the 1960s. Bernie got himself elected president and by 1978, having realised television was the sport's bedfellow, set about arranging deals.

It was Bernie, described by motor-racing journalist Alan Henry as now 'the most powerful and influential single individual in professional motor racing', who took the sport by its cockpits, shook it violently and, amongst other things, arranged those broadcasting deals worldwide which now make it possible to watch Rosberg in Rio, Mansell in Monaco, Piquet in Portugal and Boutsen in Belgium.

Two years before, though, because of a little sponsorship hiccup (see page 98), the biggest Formula One story in the UK since Jackie Stewart completed his hat-trick of Championship wins – that of James Hunt's World Championship year of 1976 – received comparatively little television

Opposite, *Ascari and Ferrari, winners of the first Grand Prix televised live by the BBC*

Motor-racing fan George Harrison listens – and FOCA President Bernie Ecclestone talks

attention. Despite the news coverage of James's triumph in Japan when Lauda quit the race, there was not the celebration of 'victory' which the 'tifosi' in Italy would have demanded.

But was that television's fault – or that of too pushy sponsors? Could it have been too ineffectual ruling bodies within the sport? Two years later, whatever the reasons, all was resolved – or nearly so – and motor racing was back on the box.

Those very early days – the Raymond Baxter era – of television, and indeed of the sport itself, would make a book in their own right. Let us therefore concentrate on the television role from its rebirth in that winter of 1978.

It never was a secret, although most viewers would probably not have realised, that Murray Walker was not actually at a Grand Prix, except for the British. That's not to say that Murray, who made his first broadcast back in 1949, wasn't at Monaco or Monza, Zolder or Zandvoort. He was – to watch the two vital practice sessions, usually on the Friday and Saturday – but he used to hot-foot it back to the relative safety of BBC Television Centre's videotape recording area underground at White City in West London.

There, on Sunday mornings, the motor-racing programme's production team, headed then by the now Head of Television Sport, Jonathan Martin, who created the *Grand Prix* programme, would wait nervously for Murray to burst through the door to watch the incoming Eurovision coverage of whichever Grand Prix he had left the day before. Murray would make notes while watching the race, then sit through the editing of the highlights (because that was all there was in those pre-*Sunday Grandstand* days). He would then dub on his commentary just before transmission – or very often, when a race was delayed or editing had been slower than normal, it would go on 'live' over the recorded pictures.

Why all the subterfuge? It was felt that this sytem yielded a more polished programme to watch. That's motor show business!

Just why did the sport 'take off' in 1978? Jonathan Martin, who also brought *Ski Sunday* to the screen, believed then that a myriad of technical advances, both in television and in the sports (both motor racing *and* skiing) made the time ripe to launch new sports programmes.

With the advent of *Sunday Grandstand* in mid-May 1981 and live coverage of Grands Prix in the afternoon, Murray's role suddenly changed. On that May day Murray found himself on site to commentate on the rain-interrupted Belgian Grand Prix, joined for the first time by the ebullient James Hunt. And from that day to this, for most of the races, that's the way it's done – Murray and James at the track reporting the race they are actually seeing in (hopefully) perfect harmony!

Of course, the BBC team comes into its own at the British Grand Prix (and, in recent years, the European Grand Prix when it has been raced in England). The other fifteen races each year are covered by the foreign broadcasters in their own countries – which could explain the variation in the quality of race television coverage! The countdown for Britain's most important race of the year begins twelve months before – immediately after the previous year's Grand Prix. After the post mortems, the planning, including several site visits to arrange new camera angles, facilities for foreign broadcasters, the sponsors' role, even on-site catering for up to 150 domestic television and Eurovision staff, for whom the pits, paddock, grandstands and track are to be home for the next five days.

What about those cameras? Well, if you include just one 'mini-cam' mounted on board a car (and more of that later), the BBC director has no fewer than fourteen different shots to look at at the same time – and that doesn't include keeping an eye on slow-motion videotape replay machines, captioning facilities and the computer (more of that as well later). Incidentally, the Channel 9 producer in Adelaide for the first Australian Grand Prix last October was originally contemplating using more than twenty cameras, because the trees around the circuit obstructed the view and the city

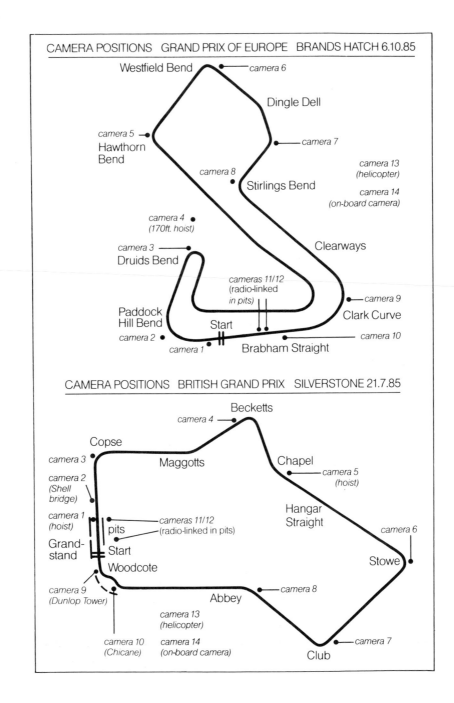

CAMERA POSITIONS   GRAND PRIX OF EUROPE   BRANDS HATCH 6.10.85

Westfield Bend — camera 6

Dingle Dell

camera 5 — Hawthorn Bend

camera 7

camera 8

Stirlings Bend

camera 13 (helicopter)

camera 14 (on-board camera)

camera 4 (170ft. hoist)

camera 3 — Druids Bend

Clearways

cameras 11/12 (radio-linked in pits)

camera 9

Paddock Hill Bend

Clark Curve

camera 2

Start

camera 10

camera 1

Brabham Straight

CAMERA POSITIONS   BRITISH GRAND PRIX   SILVERSTONE 21.7.85

Becketts

camera 4 —

Copse

camera 3

Maggotts

Chapel

camera 5 (hoist)

camera 2 (Shell bridge)

camera 1 (hoist)

cameras 11/12 (radio-linked in pits)

pits

Hangar Straight

camera 6

Grand-stand

Start

Stowe

Woodcote

camera 9 (Dunlop Tower)

camera 8

Abbey

camera 13 (helicopter)

camera 10 (Chicane)

camera 14 (on-board camera)

camera 7

Club

The punch-up at Hockenheim – captured by television: Piquet and Salazar disagree in 1982

council wouldn't let him cut them down! In the end he was persuaded that perhaps that number of cameras was a little over the top.

But back to the domestic scene. Ten of the BBC's cameras are in 'fixed' positions around the circuit, with a further two 'mobile' in the pits, another in the helicopter – and, of course, our friend the 'on-board' camera. Take about nine miles of camera and sound cables, two hoists (one of which whisks an intrepid cameraman 170 feet above the ground for spectacular aerial shots), seven radio links for transmitting vision circuits out of the track, three mobile generators to provide the power and four working days to 'rig' the lot – and you have the bare bones of what goes into televising the race.

What of the producer's role on the day? It goes something like this:
0630. He leaves his hotel twenty miles away to beat the traffic, but already

Caught by television again: Brundle's crash in practice at Monaco in 1984. Later he talked to Murray

the first of 100,000 spectators are in the circuit, scrambling for seats aboard the buses that tour the track.

0700. Breakfast alfresco in the BBC 'chuck waggon' – eggs and bacon and a chance to talk to two of the most important people around: the engineering manager, who will make it all happen technically, and Murray Walker, who will be commentating not only for viewers in the UK but also for millions more in Australia, Canada and other international zones.

0800. One of the 'mobile' cameras in the pits is released to a second producer and reporter to record material for a preview of the race – perhaps a mock pit-stop by the Brabham team.

0900. The producer, his assistant and the engineering staff climb aboard the mobile control room situated behind the main grandstand, for a final facilities check with all the staff – including cameras.

1000. Murray positions himself in front of camera nine – a 'low-angle' camera on the grandstand side of the start/finish line. He delivers an 'in vision scene set' for UK viewers, recorded by videotape engineers in London for transmission later.

1030. Untimed warm-up for the Formula One cars, which is also a last chance for the cameramen to familiarise themselves with the cars and drivers through the small black and white viewfinders mounted on top of each camera.

1115. Murray has climbed into his seat in the BBC commentary box, in the Dunlop Tower at Silverstone or on top of the new hospitality suites at

Brands Hatch. James joins him, and together they commentate on one of the earlier races, for transmission possibly a week later.

1200. The producer and reporter working on the preview take over the controls to 'voice over' the pictures they have put together.

1215. The producer calls a lunch break – but even on-site catering takes second place to the aerobatic team roaring deafeningly overhead.

1345. Back to the mobile control room. By now everyone is as keyed up as the drivers. It is 45 minutes to the green light but there is still a lot to do.

1400. One of the hand-held cameras is directed on to the grid to offer close-up pictures of the drivers. Remember Nelson Piquet's 'Hello Mum' sign? As pre-recorded pictures are seen by UK viewers, those tens of millions of people around the world join 'live' via Eurovision. Now everyone, including domestic audiences, is taking the BBC pictures. The pole man and then the rest of the grid come into view. A final visual check on the grid line-up with captions – there's the drivers' championship table and the constructors' table and, of course, the circuit map. Then the mechanics and news photographers, the cameramen and the sponsors scamper from the track and the warm-up lap begins.

1430. One final word of good luck to everyone from the producer as the cars come to a halt before the red light. Then it's a green light for the drivers and a 'Go' from Murray – and the television team's work really begins!

Two hours later it's not quite all over. There are interviews to be done, often further races to be covered. Then it's back to the hotel for the after-race discussions – both technical and emotional – and then there is next year to think about before bed.

Without doubt the most exciting – if a little gimmicky – television coverage of the most recent races has been the introduction of the 'on-board' camera. Following the 1985 Adelaide race a leading French sports magazine lamented: 'It has taken the Australians to show the world how to run cameras *in* Formula One cars.' The truth is that it was a small British firm together with a French company that developed the cigarette packet-size camera mounted on Tambay's Renault. In some ways the French journalist who wrote that story cannot be blamed because it was the Australians who pioneered the use of live on-board cameras in the now famous saloon car race at Bathurst.

Late in 1984 David Earl's Northampton-based TV2 Communications company was approached by FOCA to develop a similar system to the one he was already using in rally cars. In order to provide the broadcaster, and ultimately the viewer, with live pictures from a racing car travelling at up to 240 mph, it is necessary to transmit the signals via a microwave link to a helicopter hovering 1500 feet above the circuit. From the helicopter the pictures are retransmitted via a second link directly into the producer's mobile control van – and if 'cut up' by the producer are sent into the homes of millions of television viewers.

It takes a crew of four technicians, a helicopter pilot, hours of painstaking work, and many thousands of pounds to get the system to work. But work it nearly did at Brands Hatch in 1985 when the Grand Prix of Europe was scheduled to see the camera début. Unfortunately some 'pirate' radio signal somewhere around the circuit triggered off the remotely-controlled lens-cleaning system on the camera, which worked beautifully for one lap, using up all its cleaning fluid, and then there was nothing left to wash the lens clean for the remainder of Tambay's race.

By Adelaide the system was working perfectly but the Renault wasn't! On lap 7 the differential on poor Patrick's car went – and so did the on-board camera. One day it is the intention of both FOCA and FISA to have simultaneous live pictures from more than one car – and, who knows, possibly live driver interviews, just like Bathurst.

Now, as if the 'on-board' camera wasn't the very pinnacle of technological achievement, consider the computerised statistics made available to the teams, the race organisers, the media, the broadcasters, and therefore to you, the viewer, by Longines Olivetti, who quaintly call the service they operate a 'competition data monitoring and processing system'!

The wonderful world of the Longines/Olivetti computer – who needs a lap charter?

Developed, would you believe, from a previous joint project in World Cup skiing, the system provides, amongst other things, the race time of each competitor every time he crosses the start/finish line, the fastest lap, and the timed difference between, say, the leading car and the second-placed driver. All of which are instantly displayed on television monitors in the pits, the press room and, for television commentators, alongside the race-coverage monitors. And, of course, the information is also readily available to the television producer, who can superimpose the statistics over his race pictures to enhance a point he and the commentator are attempting to make to the viewer.

All of this might suggest that Murray's job is easy, but having just read his comments in the previous chapter you will know that is not so. Criticising the commentator is easy – just as it is easy to castigate the television coverage of a race. But remember the sport is just about the fastest-moving event to watch – and to cover. It is spread over a large area – perhaps up to three miles, sometimes winding around houses, harbours and hotels, sometimes amongst fields, forest and farmhouses. Unlike football, for example, or snooker, where the television camera basically has to follow the ball, in motor racing the television producer can be directing his camera at Hawthorn and Westfield Bends to follow the leader, whilst a mile away at

Not quite as quick as the computer: boy scouts lap-charting at Brooklands in 1922

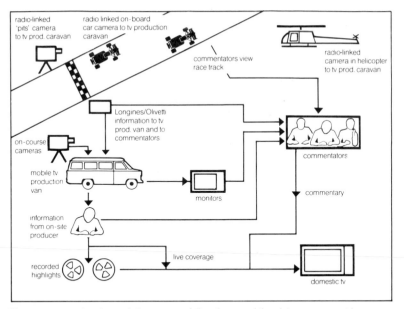

The cars go round and round, the cameras follow them, and the pictures come out here

Clark Curve someone has spun off, a back marker is in the pits, and the cars in fifth and sixth place are duelling at Druids. It is a brave/skilful/lucky man who makes the decision to 'put a camera to air' and makes a 'perfect' decision – which is why television coverage of each Grand Prix varies so much. As you have gathered, each race is covered by that country's domestic broadcaster and, as there is generally only one Grand Prix a year per country to practise on, the quality can be inconsistent. There is also the occasional problem of bias . . . !

Television has given international recognition, glory and wealth to the Grand Prix winners. Television has delivered the sponsors' image according to FOCA. Television has given the increasing number of motor-racing fans the 'ultimate' view of their sport. All of which *suggests* that Grand Prix motor racing needs television rather than the other way around. But then again, why do the television audiences worldwide continue to grow? Could it be serendipity? Or could it just be that the ultimate high-speed sport needs, demands and gets the ultimate in the 'highly skilful application of front-line technology'? Whatever the view, the 'enjoyment' factor outweighs the prejudices . . . so far!

APPENDICES

DRIVERS' WORLD CHAMPIONSHIP

1950   Giuseppe Farina, ITA (Alfa Romeo)
1951   Juan-Manuel Fangio, ARG (Alfa Romeo)
1952   Alberto Ascari, ITA (Ferrari)
1953   Ascari (Ferrari)
1954   Fangio (Maserati/Mercedes)
1955   Fangio (Mercedes)
1956   Fangio (Lancia/Ferrari)
1957   Fangio (Maserati)
1958   Mike Hawthorn, GB (Ferrari)
1959   Jack Brabham, AUS (Cooper Climax)
1960   Brabham (Cooper Climax)
1961   Phil Hill, USA (Ferrari)
1962   Graham Hill, GB (BRM)
1963   Jim Clark, GB (Lotus Climax)
1964   John Surtees, GB (Ferrari)
1965   Clark (Lotus Climax)
1966   Brabham (Brabham Repco)
1967   Denis Hulme, NZ (Brabham Repco)
1968   G. Hill (Lotus Ford)
1969   Jackie Stewart, GB (Matra Ford)
1970   Jochen Rindt, AUT (Lotus Ford)
1971   Stewart (Tyrrell Ford)
1972   Emerson Fittipaldi, BRA (Lotus Ford)
1973   Stewart (Tyrrell Ford)
1974   Fittipaldi (McLaren Ford)
1975   Niki Lauda, AUT (Ferrari)
1976   James Hunt, GB (McLaren Ford)
1977   Lauda (Ferrari)
1978   Mario Andretti, USA (Lotus Ford)
1979   Jody Scheckter, SA (Ferrari)
1980   Alan Jones, AUS (Williams Ford)
1981   Nelson Piquet, BRA (Brabham Ford)
1982   Keke Rosberg, FIN (Williams Ford)
1983   Piquet (Brabham BMW Turbo)
1984   Lauda (McLaren TAG/Porsche Turbo)
1985   Alain Prost, FRA (McLaren TAG/Porsche Turbo)

CONSTRUCTORS' WORLD CHAMPIONSHIP
Called 'Formula One Constructors'
Championship' until 1982

1958	Vanwall	1968	Lotus	1978	Lotus
1959	Cooper	1969	Matra	1979	Ferrari
1960	Cooper	1970	Lotus	1980	Williams
1961	Ferrari	1971	Tyrrell	1981	Williams
1962	BRM	1972	Lotus	1982	Ferrari
1963	Lotus	1973	Lotus	1983	Ferrari
1964	Ferrari	1974	McLaren	1984	McLaren
1965	Lotus	1975	Ferrari	1985	McLaren
1966	Brabham	1976	Ferrari		
1967	Brabham	1977	Ferrari		

Most no. of Pole Positions (to end 1985)

Clark, 33	Arnoux, 18	Prost, 15
Fangio, 28	Piquet, 18	Ascari, 14
Lauda, 24	Stewart, 17	Hunt, 14
Andretti, 18	Moss, 16	Peterson, 14

Circuits

Argentina Buenos Aires
Australia Adelaide
Austria Österreichring
Belgium Spa-Francorchamps;
  Zolder
Brazil Jacarepagua, Rio
Canada Montreal
France Paul Ricard, nr Marseilles
Germany Hockenheim;
  Nürburgring
Great Britain Brands Hatch;
  Silverstone

Holland Zandvoort
Hungary Budapest
Italy Imola; Monza
Mexico Mexico City
Monaco Monte Carlo
Portugal Estoril
San Marino Imola
South Africa Kyalami
Spain Jerez
Sweden Anderstorp
USA Dallas; Detroit; Las Vegas;
  Long Beach; Watkins Glen

DRIVERS DECLARED AT THE BEGINNING OF THE 1986 SEASON

Alain Prost (left) *and Keke Rosberg, world champions together with McLaren*

CAR NO. 1   ALAIN PROST

Nationality   French
Date of Birth   24.2.55
Lives   St Croix, Switzerland
Married   to Anne-Marie
Team   Marlboro McLaren
   International; 1981–3 Renault;
   1980 McLaren
First Grand Prix   Argentina 1980
*No. of Grands Prix (to end
1985)*   89
No. of pole positions
15 1981 Germany, Holland
   1982 Brazil, Belgium, Detroit,
   Switzerland, Las Vegas
   1983 France, Monaco, Belgium
   1984 Monaco, Germany,
   Holland
   1985 Austria, Belgium
No. of wins
21 1981 France, Holland, Italy
   1982 South Africa, Brazil
   1983 France, Belgium, Britain,
   Austria
   1984 Brazil, San Marino,
   Monaco, Germany, Holland,
   Europe, Portugal
   1985 Brazil, Monaco, Britain,
   Austria, Italy
*World Championship placings
and points*

1980 15th 5 pts
1981 5th 43 pts
1982 4th 34 pts
1983 2nd 57 pts
1984 2nd 71½ pts
1985 1st 73 pts
Favourite driver   Niki Lauda
   and Jackie Stewart
Favourite track   The one on
   which he wins!
Likes   Golf
Dislikes   His sponsor's public
   relations officer!

CAR NO. 2   KEKE ROSBERG

Nationality   Finnish
Date of Birth   6.12.48
Lives   Ibiza
Married   to Sinna
Team   Marlboro McLaren
   International; 1982–5 Williams;
   1980–1 Fittipaldi; 1978–9 Wolf;
   1978 ATS & Theodore
First Grand Prix   South Africa 1978
*No. of Grands Prix (to end
1985)*   98
No. of pole positions
4 1982 Britain
   1983 Brazil
   1985 France, Britain
No. of wins
5 1982 Switzerland
   1983 Monaco
   1984 Dallas
   1985 Detroit, Australia
*World Championship placings
and points*
1978 0 pts
1979 0 pts
1980 10th 6 pts
1981 0 pts
1982 1st 44 pts

1983 5th 27 pts
1984 8th 20½ pts
1985 3rd 40 pts
Favourite driver   None
Favourite track   None
Likes   Water sports and
   Italian food
Dislikes   Paparazzi

CAR NO. 3   MARTIN BRUNDLE

Nationality   British
Date of Birth   1.6.59
Lives   South Wooton,
   near Kings Lynn
Married   to Liz
Team   Data General Team Tyrrell
First Grand Prix   Brazil 1984
   (later declared illegally entered)
*No. of Grands Prix (to end
1985)*   22 (7 illegal)
No. of pole positions   None
No. of wins   None
*World Championship placings
and points*

1984 0 pts
1985 0 pts
Favourite driver   Jackie Stewart
Favourite track   Spa-
Francorchamps
Likes   Great Britain, all cars and
watching sport
Dislikes   Cold, rainy days

1985 15th 4 pts
Favourite driver   Alain Prost and
Jackie Stewart
Favourite track   Österreichring
Likes   All sport, particularly skiing
and water skiing
Dislikes   Getting up early on
Sundays to go motor racing

CAR NO. 4   PHILIPPE STREIFF

Nationality   French
Date of Birth   26.6.55
Lives   Neuilly
Married   to Renée
Team   Data General Team Tyrrell;
1985 Ligier & Tyrrell;
1984 Renault
First Grand Prix   Portugal 1984
No. of Grands Prix (to end 1985) 6
No. of pole positions   None
No. of wins   None
*World Championship placings
and points*
1984 0 pts

CAR NO. 5   NIGEL MANSELL

Nationality   British
Date of Birth   8.8.54
Lives   Port Erin, Isle of Man
Married   to Rosanne
Team   Canon Williams Honda;
1980–4 John Player Team Lotus
First Grand Prix   Austria 1980
*No. of Grands Prix (to end
1985)*   74
No. of pole positions
2 1984 Dallas
1985 South Africa
No. of wins
2 1985 Europe, South Africa

World Championship placings
and points
1980 0 pts
1981 14th 8 pts
1982 14th 7 pts
1983 12th 10 pts
1984 9th 13 pts
1985 6th 31 pts
Favourite driver   Jim Clark
Favourite track   Monaco
Likes   Roast dinner – and a good
   sleep afterwards
Dislikes   Queuing and traffic jams

CAR NO. 6   NELSON PIQUET

Nationality   Brazilian
Date of Birth   17.8.52
Lives   Monte Carlo
Married   divorced
Team   Canon Williams Team
   Honda; 1978–85 Brabham;
   1978 Ensign & McLaren

First Grand Prix   Germany 1978
No. of Grands Prix (to end
1985)   110
No. of pole positions
18 1980 Long Beach, Canada
   1981 Brazil, Argentina, Monaco,
   Canada
   1982 Austria
   1983 Holland
   1984 South Africa, San Marino,
   Canada, Detroit, Britain, Austria,
   Italy, Europe, Portugal
   1985 Holland
No. of wins
13 1980 Long Beach, Holland, Italy
   1981 Argentina, San Marino,
   Germany
   1982 Canada
   1983 Brazil, Italy, Europe
   1984 Canada, Detroit
   1985 France
World Championship placings
and points
1978 0 pts
1979 15th 3 pts
1980 2nd 54 pts
1981 1st 50 pts
1982 11th 20 pts
1983 1st 59 pts
1984 5th 29 pts
1985 8th 21 pts
Favourite driver   Niki Lauda
Favourite track   Österreichring
Likes   His first girl friend
Dislikes   Commercial airline travel
   and journalists

CAR NO. 7   RICCARDO
PATRESE

Nationality   Italian
Date of Birth   17.4.54
Lives   Monte Carlo

Married   single
Team   Olivetti Brabham; 1984–5
Alfa Romeo; 1982–3 Brabham;
978–81 Arrows; 1977 Shadow
First Grand Prix   Monaco 1977
*No. of Grands Prix (to end
1985)*   128
No. of pole positions
2 1981 Long Beach
1983 Italy
No. of wins
2 1982 Monaco
1983 South Africa
*World Championship placings
and points*
1977 19th 1 pt
1978 11th 11 pts
1979 19th 2 pts
1980 9th 7 pts
1981 11th 10 pts
1982 10th 21 pts
1983 9th 13 pts
1984 13th 8 pts
1985 0 pts

CAR NO. 8   ELIO DE ANGELIS
(see also p. 166)
Nationality   Italian
Date of Birth   20.3.58
Lives   Monte Carlo
Married   single
Team   Olivetti Brabham; 1980–5
John.Player Team Lotus;
1979 Shadow
First Grand Prix   Argentina 1979
*No. of Grands Prix (to end
1985)*   104
No. of pole positions
3 1983 Europe
1984 Brazil
1985 Canada
No. of wins
2 1982 Austria
1985 San Marino

*World Championship placings
and points*
1979 15th 3 pts
1980 7th 13 pts
1981 8th 14 pts
1982 9th 23 pts
1983 17th 2 pts
1984 3rd 34 pts
1985 5th 33 pts

Elio De Angelis died after an accident in testing in May 1986. A man of great culture and a pianist of near-concert level, he is sorely missed by all who knew him.

*No. of Grands Prix (to end
1985)* None
No. of pole positions None
No. of wins None
*World Championship placings
and points* None
Favourite driver Ronnie Peterson
Favourite track Hasn't got one
Likes Most sport – enjoys
watching boxing and rugby,
playing squash
Dislikes Gossip columns

CAR NO. 11 JOHNNY DUMFRIES

Nationality Scottish
Date of Birth 26.4.58
Lives North Creek, Norfolk
Married to Freddie
Team John Player Team Lotus
First Grand Prix Brazil 1986

CAR NO. 12 AYRTON SENNA

Nationality Brazilian
Date of Birth 21.3.60
Lives Esher, Surrey
Married divorced
Team John Player Team Lotus;
1984 Toleman
First Grand Prix Brazil 1984
*No. of Grands Prix (to end
1985)* 30

No. of pole positions
7 1985 Portugal, San Marino, Monaco, Detroit, Italy, Europe, Australia
No. of wins
2 1985 Portugal, Belgium
World Championship placings and points
1984 9th 13 pts
1985 4th 38 pts
Favourite driver Niki Lauda
Favourite track Portugal and Silverstone
Likes To be at home with friends and family
Dislikes To be disturbed in his private life by the press and people who do not respect his privacy

Lives Basingstoke, Hants
Married single
Team Zakspeed; 1984 RAM; 1983 Williams
First Grand Prix Europe 1983
No. of Grands Prix (to end 1985) 23
No. of pole positions None
No. of wins None
World Championship placings and points
1983 0 pts
1984 0 pts
1985 0 pts
Favourite driver Ayrton Senna
Favourite track Brands Hatch
Likes Flying helicopters
Dislikes Wasting time

CAR NO. 14 JONATHAN PALMER

Nationality British
Date of Birth 7.11.56

CAR NO. 15 ALAN JONES

Nationality Australian
Date of Birth 2.11.46
Lives London
Married to Beverley

Team Lola; 1983 Arrows;
   1978–81 Williams; 1977 Shadow;
   1976 Surtees; 1975 Hesketh
   and Lola
First Grand Prix Spain 1975
*No. of Grands Prix (to end
1985)* 100
No. of pole positions
6 1979 Britain, Canada, Watkins
   Glen
   1980 Argentina, Belgium,
   Germany
No. of wins
12 1977 Austria
   1979 Germany, Austria,
   Holland, Canada
   1980 Argentina, France, Britain,
   Canada, Watkins Glen
   1981 Long Beach, Las Vegas
*World Championship placings
and points*
1975 17th 2 pts
1976 14th 7 pts
1977 7th 22 pts
1978 11th 11 pts
1979 3rd 40 pts
1980 1st 67 pts
1981 3rd 46 pts
1983 0 pts
1985 0 pts
Favourite driver Ronnie Peterson
Favourite track All circuits
Likes Sydney oysters and Fosters
   lager
Dislikes Cold weather

CAR NO. 16 PATRICK TAMBAY

Nationality French
Date of Birth 25.6.49
Lives Villars, Switzerland and
   Wimbledon
Married to Dana

Team Lola; 1984–5 Renault;
   1982–3 Ferrari; 1981 Theodore
   and Ligier; 1978–9 McLaren;
   1977 Ensign
First Grand Prix Britain 1977
*No. of Grands Prix (to end
1985)* 100
No. of pole positions
5 1983 Long Beach; Germany;
   Austria; South Africa
   1984 France
No. of wins
2 1982 Germany
   1983 San Marino
*World Championship placings
and points*
1977 17th 5 pts
1978 13th 8 pts
1979 0 pts
1981 18th 1 pt
1982 7th 25 pts
1983 4th 40 pts
1984 11th 11 pts
1985 11th 11 pts

Favourite driver Gilles Villeneuve
Favourite track Österreichring
Likes Spaghetti and red cars!
Dislikes Slow cars

CAR NO. 17 MARC SURER

Nationality Swiss
Date of Birth 18.9.51
Lives Switzerland and Spain
Married single
Team Arrows; 1985 Brabham;
  1982–4 Arrows; 1981 Ensign &
  Theodore; 1980 ATS; 1979
  Ensign
First Grand Prix USA 1979
*No. of Grands Prix (to end
1985)* 77
No. of pole positions None
No. of wins None
*World Championship placings
and points*
1979 0 pts
1980 0 pts
1981 16th 4 pts

1982 20th 3 pts
1983 15th 4 pts
1984 21st 1 pt
1985 13th 5 pts
Favourite driver Nelson Piquet
Favourite track Brands Hatch
Likes Horse riding
Dislikes Narrow-minded people

Surer was badly injured rallying in
May 1986.

CAR NO. 18 THIERRY BOUTSEN

Nationality Belgian
Date of Birth 13.7.57
Lives Brussels
Married to Patricia
Team Arrows
First Grand Prix Belgium 1983
*No. of Grands Prix (to end
1985)* 41
No. of pole positions None
No. of wins None
*World Championship placings
and points*

1983 0 pts
1984 14th 5 pts
1985 11th 11 pts
Favourite driver   Jackie Stewart
Favourite track   Spa and Brands
    Hatch
Likes   Competition
Dislikes   The face of the world
    today – war and poverty

No. of wins   None
*World Championship placings
and points*
1982 0 pts
1984 12th 9 pts
1985 0 pts
Favourite driver   Jim Clark and
    Nelson Piquet
Favourite track, Österreichring
Likes   My family – wife and child
Dislikes   Liars

CAR NO. 19   TEO FABI

CAR NO. 20   GERHARD BERGER

Nationality   Italian
Date of Birth   9.3.55
Lives   Milan
Married   to Gloria
Team   Benetton; 1985 Toleman
    (now Benetton); 1984 Brabham;
    1982 Toleman
First Grand Prix   San Marino 1982
*No. of Grands Prix (to end
1985)*   32
No. of pole positions
1 1985 Germany

Nationality   Austrian
Date of Birth   27.8.59
Lives   Worgl, nr Innsbruck, Austria
Married   single
Team   Benetton; 1985 Arrows;
    1984 ATS
First Grand Prix   Austria 1984
*No. of Grands Prix (to end
1985)*   20
No. of pole positions   None
No. of wins   None

World Championship placings and points
1984 21st 1 pt
1985 17th 3 pts
Favourite driver   Gilles Villeneuve
Favourite track   Österreichring
Likes   Going to bed early
Dislikes   Getting up early

1981 0 pts
1982 0 pts
1983 0 pts
1984 19th 2 pts
1985 0 pts
Favourite driver   Jackie Stewart
Favourite track   Nürburgring
Likes   Body-building
Dislikes   Rugby and American football

CAR NO. 21   PIERCARLO GHINZANI

Nationality   Italian
Date of Birth   16.1.52
Lives   Monte Carlo
Married   to Angela
Team   Osella; 1985 Toleman; 1981–5 Osella
First Grand Prix   Belgium 1981
No. of Grands Prix (to end 1985)   36
No. of pole positions   None
No. of wins   None
World Championship placings and points

CAR NO. 22   CHRISTIAN DANNER

Nationality   German
Date of Birth   4.4.58
Lives   Munich
Married   single
Team   Osella; 1985 Zakspeed
First Grand Prix   Belgium 1985
No. of Grands Prix (to end 1985)   2
No. of pole positions   None
No. of wins   None
World Championship placings and points   None

Favourite driver The *style* of
  Carlos Reutemann
Favourite track Mugello
Likes Tolerant people
Dislikes Chauvinism, nationalism
  and intolerant people

CAR NO. 23 ANDREA DE
CESARIS

Nationality Italian
Date of Birth 31.5.59
Lives Rome
Married single
Team Minardi; 1984–5 Ligier;
  1982–3 Alfa Romeo; 1981
  McLaren; 1980 Alfa Romeo
First Grand Prix Canada 1980

*No. of Grands Prix (to end
1985)* 73
No. of pole positions
1 Long Beach
No. of wins None
*World Championship placings
and points*
1980 0 pts
1981 18th 1 pt
1982 17th 5 pts
1983 8th 15 pts
1984 16th 3 pts
1985 17th 3 pts
Favourite driver Niki Lauda
Favourite track Spa
Likes Auto-cross
Dislikes Being away from home
  for long periods

De Cesaris (left) *finds life funny: Nannini takes a more sober look at the Minardi scene*

CAR NO. 24 ALESSANDRO NANNINI

Nationality Italian
Date of Birth 7.7.59
Lives Siena
Married single
Team Minardi
First Grand Prix Brazil 1986
No. of Grands Prix (to end 1985) None
No. of pole positions None
No. of wins None
World Championship placings and points None
Favourite driver Juan-Manuel Fangio
Favourite track Imola and Monza
Likes Sun, swimming and sleep
Dislikes Work

Married divorced
Team Ligier; 1983–5 Ferrari; 1979–82 Renault; 1978 Martini and Surtees
First Grand Prix Belgium 1978
No. of Grands Prix (to end 1985) 96
No. of pole positions
18 1979 Austria, Holland
1980 Austria, Holland, Italy
1981 France, Britain, Austria, Italy
1982 South Africa, San Marino, Monaco, Holland, France
1983 San Marino, Detroit, Canada, Britain
No. of wins
7 1980 Brazil, South Africa
1982 France, Italy
1983 Canada, Germany, Holland
World Championship placings and points
1978 0 pts
1979 8th 17 pts
1980 6th 29 pts
1981 9th 11 pts
1982 6th 28 pts
1983 3rd 49 pts
1984 6th 27 pts
1985 17th 3 pts
Favourite driver Jackie Stewart
Favourite track Österreichring
Likes Vintage sports cars
Dislikes Politics

CAR NO. 25 RENÉ ARNOUX

Nationality French
Date of Birth 4.7.48
Lives London

World Championship placings
and points
1974 0 pts
1975 12th 6 pts
1976 7th 20 pts
1977 10th 18 pts
1978 8th 19 pts
1979 4th 36 pts
1980 4th 34 pts
1981 4th 44 pts
1982 17th 5 pts
1983 11th 11 pts
1984 14th 5 pts
1985 9th 16 pts
Favourite driver   Alain Prost
Favourite track   Österreichring
Likes   Golf, tennis and fishing
Dislikes   Partying

CAR NO. 26   JACQUES LAFFITE

Nationality   French
Date of Birth   21.11.43
Lives   Stoke Poges, Bucks
Married   to Bernadette
Team   Ligier; 1983–4 Williams;
   1976–82 Ligier; 1975
   Williams; 1974 ISO
First Grand Prix   Germany 1974
*No. of Grands Prix (to end
1985)*   167
No. of pole positions
7 1976 Italy
   1979 Argentina, Brazil, Spain,
   Belgium
   1980 France
   1981 Spain
No. of wins
6 1977 Sweden
   1979 Argentina, Brazil
   1980 Germany
   1981 Austria, Canada

CAR NO. 27   MICHELE
ALBORETO

Nationality   Italian
Date of Birth   23.12.56
Lives   Monte Carlo

Married to Nadia
Team Ferrari; 1981–3 Tyrrell
First Grand Prix San Marino 1981
No. of Grands Prix (to end 1985) 73
No. of pole positions
2 1984 Belgium
  1985 Brazil
No. of wins
5 1982 Las Vegas
  1983 Detroit
  1984 Belgium
  1985 Canada, Germany
World Championship placings and points
1981 0 pts
1982 7th 25 pts
1983 12th 10 pts
1984 4th 30½ pts
1985 2nd 53 pts
Favourite driver Jackie Stewart
Favourite track No particular favourite, but likes Monaco, Monza, Zeltweg, Imola and Silverstone
Likes Spaghetti Bolognese, spy stories and playing tennis
Dislikes Violence

World Championship placings and points
1983 0 pts
1984 16th 3 pts
1985 7th 26 pts
Favourite driver Niki Lauda
Favourite track Silverstone and Brands Hatch
Likes Life!
Dislikes Fish

CAR NO. 28 STEFAN JOHANSSON

Nationality Swedish
Date of Birth 8.9.56
Lives London
Married single
Team Ferrari; 1985 Tyrrell; 1984 Toleman and Tyrrell; 1983 Spirit
First Grand Prix British 1983
No. of Grands Prix (to end 1985) 26
No. of pole positions None
No. of wins None

CAR NO. 29 HUUB ROTHENGATTER

Nationality Dutch
Date of Birth 8.10.54
Lives Hilversum
Married single
Team Zakspeed; 1984 Spirit; 1985 Osella
First Grand Prix Canada 1984
No. of Grands Prix (to end 1985) 14
No. of pole positions None
No. of wins None

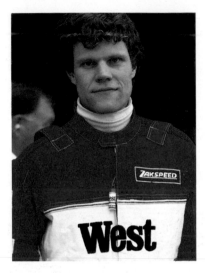

World Championship placings
and points
1984 0 pts
1985 0 pts
Favourite driver   Tazio Nuvolari
Favourite track   Original
   Nürburgring
Likes   Autobahns because there
   are no speed limits
Dislikes   Jokes about being too tall
   for Formula One

CAR NO. 8   DEREK WARWICK

Nationality   British
Date of Birth   7.8.54
Lives   Jersey
Married   to Rhonda
Team   Olivetti Brabham; 1984–5
   Renault; 1981–Toleman
First Grand Prix   Las Vegas 1981
*No. of Grands Prix (to end
   1985)*   58
No. of pole positions   None

No. of wins   None
World Championship placings
and points
1981 0 pts
1982 0 pts
1983 14th 9 pts
1984 7th 23 pts
1985 13th 5 pts
Favourite driver   Jim Clark, Rindt
   and Niki Lauda
Favourite track   Brands Hatch and
   Mugello
Likes   Going out in pleasant
   company
Dislikes   Some of the people one
   has to suffer in motor racing

FORMULA ONE'S FOUR MOST IMPORTANT MEN

BERNIE ECCLESTONE

President of the Formula One Constructors' Association, owner of the
Brabham team, former racing
driver, property millionaire and,
some say, the single most powerful
man in Grand Prix motor racing.

JEAN MARIE BALESTRE

French-born President of FISA – the
governing body world-wide of all
motor sport. He is arguably the
'second most powerful man in
Grand Prix motor racing' – although
he might dispute that lowly position!

DEREK ONGARO

Official race starter at *all* Grands Prix
since 1977 and responsible for
track safety at all Grand Prix circuits
– a FISA appointed official.

PROFESSOR SID WATKINS

Official in charge of all matters
medical at every Grand Prix circuit –
a consultant neuro-surgeon based
in London – a FOCA and FISA
appointee.

GLOSSARY OF RACING TERMS

pit garage, workshop area

paddock area, usually immediately behind pits, where car transporters, motor homes, tyre manufacturers, etc. are located

grid formation of cars at start of race, usually in two side-by-side rows of 13 each, and usually alongside pits

pole position first place on the grid, earned by fastest time in official qualifying

chicane obstacle, usually in bend of track, round which cars have to race and which serves to slow pace of race

skirt name given to Colin Chapman's invention of side panels added to bottom of cars to increase downforce and therefore speed – and now illegal

monocoque one-piece chassis

wing Inverted aerofoil giving added downforce

wets special grooved tyres for wet-weather use

slicks smooth-compound tyres, in a range of finishes (e.g. 'A' for the hardest, 'E' for the stickiest)

screamer very quick car

Dog car the driver doesn't think a lot of . . .

ace exceptionally fast driver

hot shoe man currently rated quickest of the up-and-coming drivers

rookie new driver

brain-fade driver error

closing the door making life difficult for a driver trying to overtake

shutting the gate as above – also known as baulking

out of shape getting the car on to the incorrect line, e.g. through a corner

in the groove opposite of the above

to have a moment to come close to an accident, either by losing control of the car or by tangling with another

shunt crash

wrench mechanic

truckie driver of the transporter; may also look after spares

gofer lowest of low member of team who has to 'go . . . fer' this and 'go . . . fer' that

ACKNOWLEDGEMENTS

The list of people in the Grand Prix world who have offered help and generous advice would add another chapter to this book. We hope the others will forgive us, then, if we make special mention of the following: Derick Allsop, Grand Prix correspondent of the *Daily Mail*; Ann Bradshaw, former Press Officer of the RAC Motor Sports Association; Mike Doodson, regular contributor to a host of racing magazines and other publications; Maurice Hamilton, Grand Prix correspondent of the *Guardian* and editor of *Autocourse*; Alan Henry of *Motoring News*; John Horton; Tony Hutchings, Archivist of the Brooklands Society; *Marlboro Grand Prix Guide*; Steven Tee of LAT Photographic; John Townsend of Formula One Pictures; former British Grand Prix winner John Watson; and the Formula One Constructors' Association. The authors are delighted to acknowledge their debt to Roger Chown and Tony Kingsford, and last but not least to Ann Thompson, designer of this book.

PICTURE CREDITS